Dr. Mary C. Howard

Turning Struggles Into Successes

Helping Struggling Students be Successful Readers

Reading Connections Publishing
PO Box 52426
Tulsa, Oklahoma 74152-0426
918-744-8698
www.drmaryhoward.com
mhoward@drmaryhoward.com

Turning Struggles into Successes: An Educators Guide to Helping Struggling Students Become More Successful Readers / Mary C. Howard

Published by Reading Connections
PO Box 52426
Tulsa, OK 74152-0426
Phone: (918) 744-8698
Fax: (918) 744-1052
www.drmaryhoward.com
mhoward@drmaryhoward.com

Copyright © 2004 by Dr. Mary C. Howard

All rights reserved; no part of this publication may be reproduced, stored in a retrieval system, or transmitted, in any form or by any means, electronic, mechanical, photocopying, recording, or otherwise, without the prior written permission of Reading Connections Publishing. Permission is given to make copies of student forms only for your own classroom use.

Printed in the United States of America

ISBN 0-9742877-0-9 (Book)
ISBN 0-9742877-1-7 (Book & 4 CDs)
ISBN 0-9742877-2-5 (Book & DVD)

LCCN: 2003095516

Howard, Mary C., 1950-

1. Effective Teaching 2. Reading Instruction 3. Elementary grades 4. Literacy

Cover Model: Brittyn Howard
Editor: Tracey Carreon
Coordinator: Alan Gadney (One-on-One Book Production and Marketing)
Cover Graphic Designer: Carolyn Porter
Graphic Designer (Ads & order form): Christopher West
Cover Photographer: Bill Shoemaker Photography
Photographer (Dr. Mary Howard): Tim Heit Photography
CD/DVD Duplication: Chris Lingana (Spectrum Media Group)
Clip art images ©2004 www.clipart.com

A Note to the reader: This seminar is designed to enhance the existing literacy program rather than to replace it. My goal is to highlight specific critical components of literacy instruction and to provide varied strategy suggestions to support teachers in that process. Every strategy can be adapted to fit any grade level or instructional context and can be integrated into all curriculum areas. The suggestions contained in this book are not intended to stand alone or to be used *in place of* the grade level or district curriculum, but to enrich and extend it.

DEDICATION

This book is dedicated

to the loving memory of my father,

Col. James S. Howard

for teaching me that anything is possible

and for instilling in me a love of teaching *and* learning.

and

to my mother, Sue Howard

who continues to demonstrate every day of my life

what true love is!

Thank you for teaching me that our differences make us special.

You saw my uniqueness as a gift

and gave me a passion for seeking the gifts in my students.

If only the lives of *all* children could be so richly blessed,

the possibilities would be endless!

With special love and thanks to my niece, Brittyn Howard.
You make the most beautiful cover any author has ever had.
I love you!

Acknowledgments

So many people have had an impact in making this book a reality. I am indebted to the expertise of the many educators who filled my head and heart with information to support my ongoing passion for struggling learners. To Marie Clay and the Reading Recovery program for helping me to understand that teaching always begins with the child and that the best teacher's guide is knowledge; to Dr. Richard Allington, Alfie Kohn and Susan O'Hanian for courageously *taking the heat* for those of us who are the lucky benefactors of their dedication and honesty in the name of children; to Dr. Harry Wong for getting me started in the right direction in those early days of my teaching and continuing to inspire me daily; to knowledgeable educators such as Timothy Rasinsky, P. David Pearson, Pat Wolfe, Eric Jensen and so many others who have helped to fine-tune my teaching skills; and to Dr. Mel Levine who serves as a constant reminder about what is truly important in teaching.

It takes many people to bring a book to print. Special thanks to Alan Gadney of One-on-One Book Production and Marketing for making this process a pleasurable one that finally made sense. My appreciation to graphic designer, Carolyn Porter, of One-On-One Book Production and Marketing and photographer, Bill Shoemaker, for the cover of my dreams. Thanks to photographer, Tim Heit, for providing my photograph for the book and to Tracy Carreon for providing respectful editing advice. My appreciation to www.clipart.com for the graphics that put the finishing touches on my book. Special thanks to Andy Gilliam for creating an amazing audio and video seminar while making the process such a joy. His expertise and the kindness shown to me by Andy and his lovely wife, Gail, are appreciated more than I can say. Thanks to Chris Lingana of Spectrum Media for his warmth and professionalism during the CD/DVD duplication process. Special thanks to Sister Mary Claire and the wonderful staff of Monte Cassino School in Tulsa, Oklahoma for taking part as my audience.

This project could never have come together without friends and family. I am so grateful to Matt Smith and Carla Guida of IronClad Technologies and graphic designer, Christopher West, who have supported my every technology need, no matter how short the notice. Their loyalty and friendship has been a gift. Special thanks to Dee Hinderliter, Natalie Ford and Cecelia Elliott, caregivers extraordinaire, and to Jyl and Andrew Garrean of Home Instead, for giving me peace of mind during those many hours of writing away from my precious mother and light of my life. Thanks to my niece, Brittyn, for gracing my cover and to my brothers Jim, Mike and John Howard and sister-in-laws Susan, Tracey and Mary for the many suggestions. Of course, thanks to my nieces and nephews for serving as my constant teaching inspirations.

Most of all, I am indebted in so many ways to my sister, Sandy Knox. I am eternally grateful for her unwavering love and support every day of my life. She is my sister, closest friend, collaborator, sounding board and the best assistant a working girl could have. The hours she spends listening to my ideas, concerns and frustrations inspires me daily to be the best I can be in every way. She is and always will be the best half of my personal *dream team*!

Dear Colleague,

In many ways, this book was an inevitable process that began more than forty-five years ago when educational institutions first categorized me as *different*. With a brain and body rarely at rest and a need for a constant dose of repetition, movement, visuals, and multi sensory learning, my first twelve years of schooling is little more than a painful memory. Reading seemed insurmountable, with few accommodations made for my unique style of learning. These personal experiences as a frustrated learner have since resulted in a passion for supporting struggling readers. This passion continues to be the driving force in a never-ending quest to create rich literacy programs that nurture *every* child.

I have spent the past thirty years immersing myself in the research on reading in an attempt to identify the most critical aspects of learning for struggling readers. Aware that every moment counts and that scripted programs, "cutesy" cut and paste activities and clever thematic units are not in the best interest of children already behind, I saw the same key components rising out of the best research. This research continuously reinforced my strong belief about what is most important and has served as the foundation of my seminars throughout the years. Dr. Richard Allington's remarkable book, *What Really Matters for Struggling Readers*, further secured my commitment to these factors. Over the years, I have modified and elaborated on those key components and integrated my rich teaching experiences, personal struggles and the vast research available to create a seminar that will become a remarkable resource for teachers working with struggling readers.

This book is divided into two sections, each directed at the most important aspects of literacy instruction for struggling students. The first section focuses on *five critical considerations* related to connected texts. The second section explores *six maxims for word learning* to build a strong word base through sight vocabulary and sound analysis. Using these components as a starting point, a wide repertoire of strategies is suggested for working toward each one. These highly engaging strategies are designed to make the teaching-learning process more powerful *and* pleasurable for struggling readers by incorporating all learning modalities and activating multiple memory pathways through color, visuals, drama, movement and repetition.

This book is a celebration of teaching and learning and reflects my strong conviction that teachers are the *key* to making a difference in the learning lives of children for whom traditional approaches are not working. This requires thoughtful decision-making on a day-to-day and child-to-child basis. My ultimate goal is to return control to the proper source by prioritizing children over publishers and scripted guides. The plight of struggling students will not change as long as so much faith is placed in those more motivated by sales than student need. By assuming responsibility for instructional decisions based on children over the dictates of publishers, teachers offer children a *gift*. This is the gift that guarantees successful academic experiences on a journey of lifelong learning, a journey that should be a joyous one for *every* child. Thank you for the opportunity to accompany you on the road to turning struggles into successes.

My Journey to Developing a User-Friendly Workbook

This book is more than the result of my extensive experience, study and passion for literacy. It is an accumulation of a large body of study on the brain and learning and reflects my personal journey to maximize my seminars by gazing through the eyes of a learner. As a frequent participant at educational seminars, I became painfully aware of my role *on the other side* and began to more closely inspect seminar leaders, reflecting on the behaviors that supported or deterred my learning.

This new role as *detective* led me to believe that the manner in which the information was presented was critical. My attention seemed to fade at the least opportune times, regardless of my interest in the topic. Often, small group interactions only worsened my frustration as they failed to address my waning attention *during* learning and made me feel embarrassed or uncomfortable by forcing me to verbalize my thinking before I was ready. I appreciated seminars that minimized interruptions to brief sharing opportunities throughout the day while encouraging me to connect with the material in my own way. These wise leaders respected my need to opt to review my notes or sit quietly for a moment of introspection as an alternative to small group discussion. I sought to find a way to maximize attention throughout the learning process so that the brief sharing periods I scheduled throughout the day would be more powerful and less threatening.

Armed with a strong desire to modify the way I structured my seminars, I set out to find a way to make them more interactive in nature. I recalled reading about a procedure years ago referred to as the *closure activity* and decided to adapt it as the foundation of my book. I have modified this approach extensively over the years by reflecting on my experiences as a national literacy consultant and using suggestions of participants across the country. I created a visual framework to serve as an overview of each strategy, using appealing graphics as a hook (©2004 www.clipart.com). This gave teachers a more active role in the process by translating learning in a graphic form throughout the course of the seminar. Thousands of teachers have responded positively, but have suggested that a simple step-by-step description after the visual would reinforce learning for elaboration later. This resulted in *Strategy at a Glance*, a single page description to accompany each visual.

The response to this additional component has been so positive that I felt compelled to add one more suggestion. Thousands of teachers have expressed the need to listen to the information several times, so I have made an audio and video program available to allow for repetition and multiple exposure that will live beyond the initial learning. I am so grateful to the many suggestions of dedicated teachers across the country and am honored to be able to share my passion for children and literacy in this way. This book is an acknowledgement of my great respect for educators who continue to make personal and professional growth a high priority on a daily basis. Thank you for allowing me to play a small part in that wonderful quest!

Table of Contents

Finding a Common Ground

The *Big Picture*	1
100/100 Goal/What Does Really Matter?	2
Simple Truths to Guide Literacy Instruction	3
Mary's Simple Test	4
Qualities of Effective Teachers	5
Flexible Grouping Contexts	6
Maxims for Effective Grouping	7
Characteristics of Successful Intervention	8

Big Picture Part 1: Critical Considerations for Text Reading — 9

Critical Consideration #1	10
The Text Challenge	11
Creating a Classroom Library	12
Organizing Texts for Independent Reading	14
Invitations to Reading (visual for Book Blessing/Personality Reading)	15
Strategy-at-a-Glance: Book Blessing	16
Strategy-at-a-Glance: Personality Reading	17
Personality Reading Forms	18
Reflective Pause #1	20
Critical Consideration #2	21
Assessing Fluency	22
Classroom Contexts for Building Fluency	23
Poetry Quilt	24
Personal Friendly Folder	25
Transparency Story (visual)	26
Strategy-at-a-Glance: Transparency Story	27
Transparency Story Planning Forms	28
Foot Books (visual)	30
Strategy-at-a-Glance: Foot Books	31
Reflective Pause #2	32
Critical Consideration #3	33
Creating Safety Nets & Anchors	34
The Visual Hook	42
Worksheets: Neurological Dead End Streets	43
Reflective Pause #3	44
Critical Consideration #4	45
Balancing Text Needs	46

Text Selection Categories	47
My Personal Selections Form	48
Stretch a Sentence (visual)	49
Strategy-at-a-Glance: Stretch a Sentence	50
Stretch a Sentence Form	51
Stretch a Story (visual)	52
Strategy-at-a-Glance: Stretch a Story	53
Stretch a Story Form	54
Stretch an Idea (visual)	55
Strategy-at-a-Glance: Stretch an Idea	56
Stretch an Idea Form	57
Reflective Pause #4	58
Critical Consideration #5	59
Comprehension Keys	60
Considerations for Effective Questioning	61
Questioning Prompts	62
My Strategy Bookmark	63
A Changing Focus	64
My Self-Questioning Form	65
Question Tree (visual)	66
Questioning Categories	67
Strategy-at-a-Glance: Question Tree	68
Question Tree Form	69
Buddy Questions (visual)	70
Strategy-at-a-Glance: Buddy Questions	71
Buddy Question Forms	72
Quick Tapes (visual)	74
Strategy-at-a-Glance: Quick Tapes	75
Quick Tape Form	76
Reflective Pause #5	77
Taking a Trip Down Memory Lane	78
Big Picture Part 2: Maxims for Word Learning	**79**
Making Words Memorable/High Priority Words	80
Enhancing Word Learning: Maxim 1	81
Learning By a Foot (visual)	82
Strategy-at-a-Glance: Learning by a Foot	83
Drastic Strategy (visual)	84
Strategy-at-a-Glance: Drastic Strategy	85
Reflective Pause #1	86

Enhancing Word Learning: Maxim 2	87
Fluency Practice Maze (visual)	88
Strategy-at-a-Glance: Fluency Practice Maze	89
Spelling Fluency Folder (visual)	90
Strategy-at-a-Glance: Spelling Fluency Folder	91
My Word Learning Contract	93
Reflective Pause #2	94
Enhancing Word Learning: Maxim 3	95
Memory Cards/Memory Chart (visual)	96
Strategy-at-a-Glance: Memory Cards	97
Strategy-at-a-Glance: Memory Chart	98
Memory Chart Planning Form	99
Reflective Pause #3	100
Enhancing Word Learning: Maxim 4	101
Patterns for Word Learning/Common Onsets & Rimes	102
Ways to Categorize Words/Word Maker Cups (visual)	103
Strategy-at-a-Glance: Word Maker Cups	104
Reading Round Up (visual)	105
Strategy-at-a-Glance: Reading Round Up	106
Reading Round Up Form	108
Reflective Pause #4	110
Enhancing Word Learning: Maxim 5	111
Sentence-a-Day (visual)	112
Strategy-at-a-Glance: Sentence a Day (Reading the Desk)	113
Sample Parent Letter (Sentence a Day)	115
Sample Sentence Buddy Letter (Sentence a Day)	117
Sentence Buddy Tutoring Guide	118
Sentence Buddy Response Form	119
Strategy-at-a-Glance: Connected Sentences	120
Buddy Sentences Form	121
Reflective Pause #5	122
Enhancing Word Learning: Maxim 6	123
Personal Partner Pockets (visual)	124
Strategy-at-a-Glance: Personal Partner Pockets	125
Personal Partner Pocket Forms	126
Living Posters (visual)	128
Strategy-at-a-Glance: Living Posters	129
Reflective Pause #6	130
Taking a Trip Down Memory Lane	131
Resources Cited	132
Note taking Pages	133

Much of the clipart in this book is

©2004 www.clipart.com

I highly recommend this site for educators.

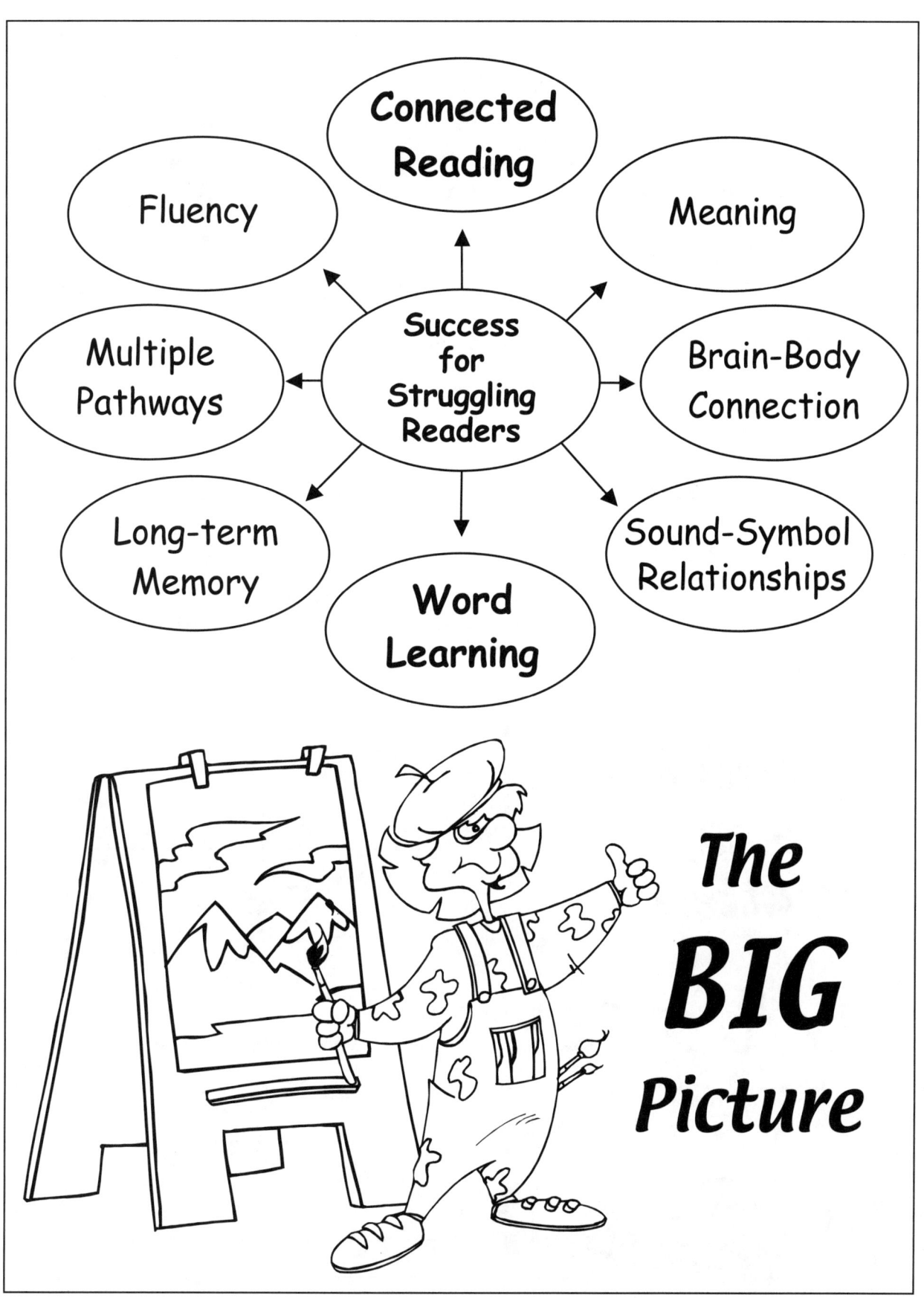

The 100/100 Goal

Imagine that we could design schools where 100% of the students were involved in instruction appropriate to their needs and development 100% of the day. Imagine how different the achievement patterns of struggling readers might be. I will suggest that the 100/100 goal is, perhaps, the real solution for developing schools that better serve struggling readers.

What Really Matters For Struggling Readers
Richard Allington; Longman (2000)

What Does Really Matter?

P _____

P _____

that

P _____

P _____

P _____

Simple Truths to Guide Literacy Instruction

All children are capable and qualified learners,
bringing a wonderful uniqueness to the educational environment.

No child is capable and qualified in *all* areas;
every strength lays a powerful framework for new learning.

You do not get to *choose* the areas of capabilities,
only to nurture and support them.

Some capabilities lay dormant, waiting beneath the surface
for just the right experiences to *awaken* them.

Educational experiences that maximize capabilities vary
and should be modified to fit unique needs on a daily basis.

While literacy *is* a developmental process,
each child has a unique timetable that should respected.

Children should be viewed in terms of *capabilities*,
rather than perceived through school-induced disabilities.

Instruction must begin with a *strong foundation*,
identifying and building on gaps in critical experiences.

Instructional opportunities can nurture or inhibit learning,
so *children always take priority over curriculum and programs.*

Begin with what *each* child brings to the table,
recognizing that *every* child brings a wealth of unique knowledge.

Search for, enrich, and celebrate the gifts of *each* child,
for they are too precious to squander!

Feeling courageous (and honest)? Take Mary's simple test...

Do you really want to know if you're an effective literacy teacher? First, be sure you're looking in the right place for the answer to that question. Don't look at the results of standardized testing, for scores may reflect good teaching but do not guarantee it. Don't look at your ability to carry out the mandates of programs, for good teachers do not need permission from others to do the right thing (which is often not in the teacher's guide). Don't look at your strongest students as a reflection of your teaching, for some children learn *in spite of* the poor choices teachers make. If you are dedicated enough and courageous enough to answer this question, take my simple test:

• Do you use programs as a resource rather than the final word, making personal decisions based on the individual needs of students?

• Are you looking for the quick fix or are you wise enough to recognize that there is no recipe that works for every child?

• Do you view yourself as a teacher of unique individuals rather than the puppet of a grade level curriculum or instructional package?

• Do you waste valuable time teaching to the test or do you teach test-taking strategies that will last a lifetime?

• Do you recognize that the volume of authentic reading and writing is the single greatest contributor to literacy development?

• Do you provide respectful texts and tasks or expect children to suffer through painful experiences that hinder success?

• Do you maintain a proper perspective, providing skill instruction while resisting the temptation to substitute it for real literacy events?

• Do you show the widest gain in the weakest readers by modifying your teaching to fit the unique learning needs of *all* children?

Qualities of Effective Teachers

Many researchers have recently explored the qualities of exemplary teachers with findings that reflect tremendous variation in the approaches and programs used. This clearly demonstrates that it is not the program or approach that makes a teacher exemplary, but the way each teacher views and addresses learning. Exemplary teachers focus on students over programs, flexibly using a variety of rich resources most appropriate for meeting the unique needs of *each* child at that time. Without exception, teachers *make the difference!*

- Show the widest gain in the weakest readers
- Use a wide repertoire of flexible strategies
- Offer varied grouping to fit learning needs and goals
- Provide flexible small group instruction
- Teach strategies in meaningful literacy contexts
- Expect high on-task behaviors
- Combine direct/indirect instruction
- Focus on process over product
- Select appropriate texts and tasks
- Teach children over curriculum
- Emphasize high level questions on a daily basis
- Maintain high expectations for *all* children
- View teaching as a lifelong learning process
- Demonstrate joyful enthusiasm *every* day

Flexible Grouping Contexts

A variety of grouping experiences are necessary in order to accommodate for the unique learning needs that exist in *every* classroom. Each grouping format serves a specific purpose, with one more desirable than another in a particular context. Research shows that the most effective teachers offer a wide variety of flexible grouping opportunities, making decisions daily based on the individual needs of students.

Whole group opportunities celebrate what each child brings to the learning community through a common experience. This may include high support strategies such as shared or modeled reading or content area learning. These supports allow every child to successfully participate regardless of current reading achievement. Whole group reading experiences are presented *through the eyes* (reading comprehension) using easy or familiar texts or *through the ears* (listening comprehension), employing activities such as read aloud and content area learning. Formal reading instruction, however, does not occur in this setting as a single text does not exist that is appropriate for all students.

Independent literacy experiences allow students to practice learning in progress through self-selected reading and writing opportunities. These opportunities reinforce what children already know and highlight what it means to be a reader by emphasizing the role literacy plays in our lives. Effective teachers build independent literacy into every school day, recognizing that *why* is equally as important as *how*. The question is no longer, *"Can we afford the time?"* but *"How can we afford not to take this time?"*

Collaboration provides opportunities for learning to occur with a partner or in small groups based on interest. Collaboration includes discussion groups, buddy reading, literature circles or extension activities that follow a text children have read on their own or with teacher support. These groups are self-selected, with varying supports offered so all students can participate successfully, regardless of reading level. In literature circles, for example, children may listen to a recorded version before meeting in the group.

Small group instruction is the heart of the reading program, including shared and guided reading experiences. The most effective teachers do *more* small group instruction because they realize that these are powerful contexts that will more readily accommodate the use of appropriate texts. They are also aware that groups must be *flexible and dynamic* to be effective, forming and reforming them on the basis of ongoing assessment rooted in the context of literacy. Two to six children at a similar instructional level read a text selected to balance comfort and challenge (90% to 94% accuracy). This allows the teacher to support students on a one-to-one basis during engaged reading, in order to reinforce effective strategies and prompt for new ones. In this way, instruction can be modified to meet individual needs using carefully selected texts over grade level packages.

Maxims for Effective Grouping

Each of these grouping variations are valuable in a different context, always selected on the basis of teacher decision-making. Modifying the setting allows teachers to adapt and orchestrate the instructional environment to meet the needs of students in a variety of ways. This is not an *either-or proposition* as each option has a specific purpose and can be valuable under the right conditions. Several maxims can be helpful in designing effective contexts for literacy:

> learning can occur in many contexts
>
> each setting has value in the right circumstances
>
> children need a variety of experiences
>
> whole group is not an effective context for reading instruction
>
> the level of text difficulty is the key
>
> guided and shared reading are the heart of the reading program
>
> reading instruction occurs in small group settings
>
> grouping is always flexible and temporary
>
> grouping decisions are based on current achievement
>
> groups are formed and reformed on a regular basis
>
> ongoing and varied assessment informs grouping decisions

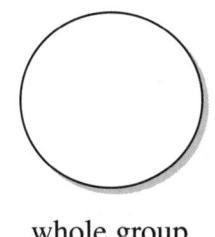

whole group opportunities (varied)

collaborative groups (self-selected)

independent literacy (self-selected)

small group instruction (teacher-selected)

Characteristics of Successful Intervention

- Instruction is designed to *support* rather than *sort* children.
- The regular classroom teacher has primary responsibility for *all* children.
- Special programs extend and support rather than *supplant* instruction.
- *Experiences* are always considered over a perceived *ability*.
- Instructional opportunities are designed to accelerate rather than remediate.
- Every moment is viewed as a valuable opportunity, so time is never wasted.
- A variety of grouping options are offered in appropriate contexts.
- Small group opportunities are emphasized for instructional purposes.
- Instructional groups are flexible, changing regularly as children progress.
- The curriculum is seen as a resource to guide rather than dictate instruction.
- Instructional decisions are based on the needs of children, not programs.
- Effective professional development is offered through ongoing support.
- Appropriate texts are selected to reinforce and support learning.
- Scaffolds and supportive frameworks are in place to guarantee success.
- Authentic reading and writing opportunities are viewed as a high priority.
- Children are *active participants* rather than *passive recipients* of learning.
- Both direct and indirect instruction are considered critical to learning.
- Instructional activities focus on teaching *strategies* over assigning tasks.
- The strengths each child brings to literacy are emphasized and highlighted.
- Instruction accommodates individual learning needs at *all* times.
- The parent/teaching relationship is viewed as a valuable *partnership*.

Big Picture

Part 1:

Critical Considerations for Connected Texts

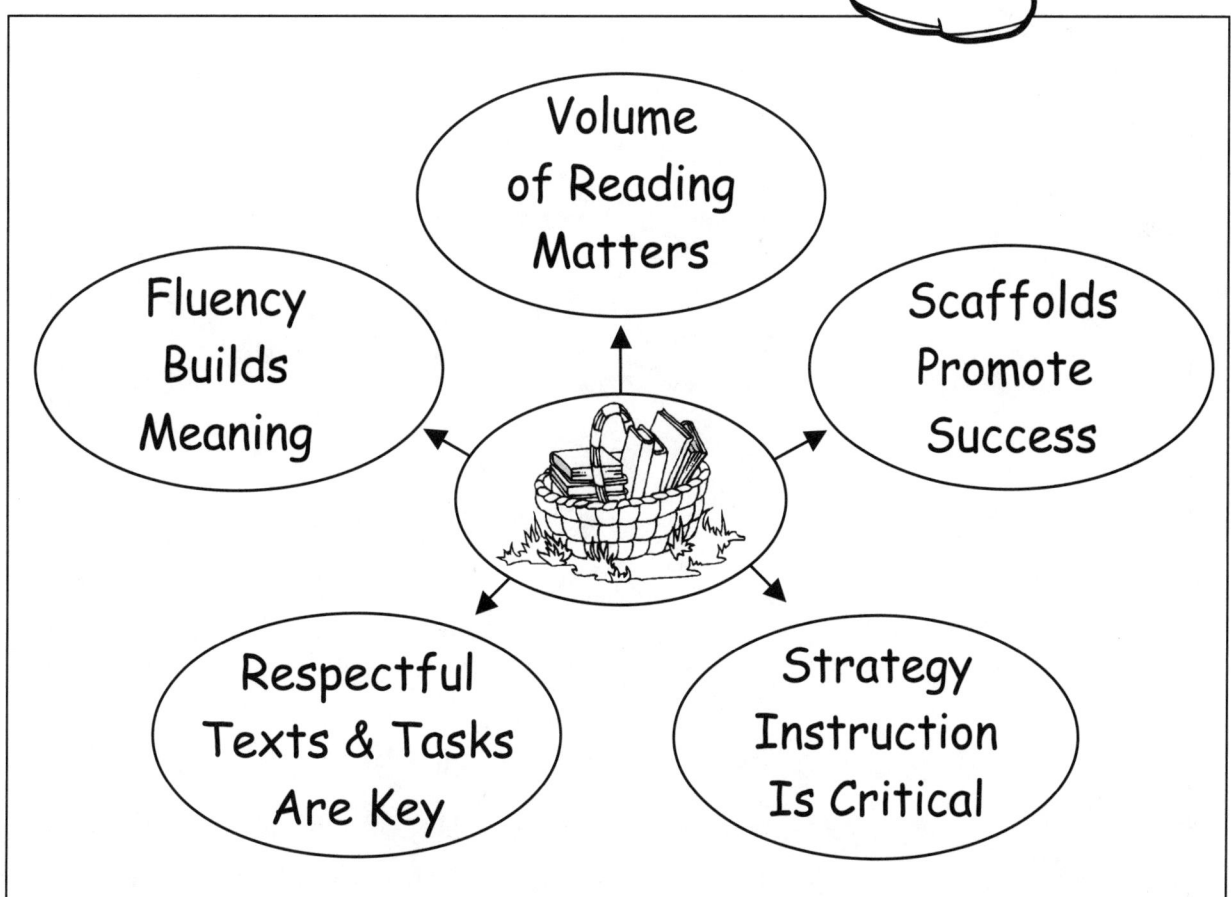

Critical Consideration #1

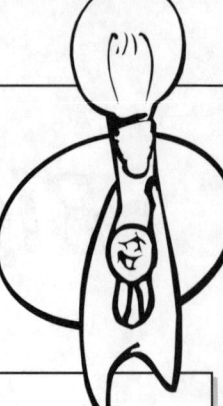

Make reading & writing a _____ .

Common sense dictates that rich resources are essential components of literacy. Yet, teachers often cite the lack of texts as their single biggest challenge. At a recent IRA conference, Richard Allington described an example of the questionable decision-making that seems to be all too common: a district allocated a meager $300 of its $110,000 budget for student books, while $72,000 was designated for computers and software. Priorities are clearly out of balance when districts scurry to purchase expensive programs and packages that are often ineffective while virtually ignoring the things that matter. Sadly, students suffer most from these inequities.

While budget constraints are a legitimate problem, it is time to equal the playing field by placing emphasis on securing appropriate texts and putting them in the hands of children. In the meantime, other text sources such as garage sales, libraries, book clubs and community resources can be explored. Variety is essential, including books appropriate for pleasurable *and* instructional purposes. Many rich resources should be accessible to this end:

The Text Challenge

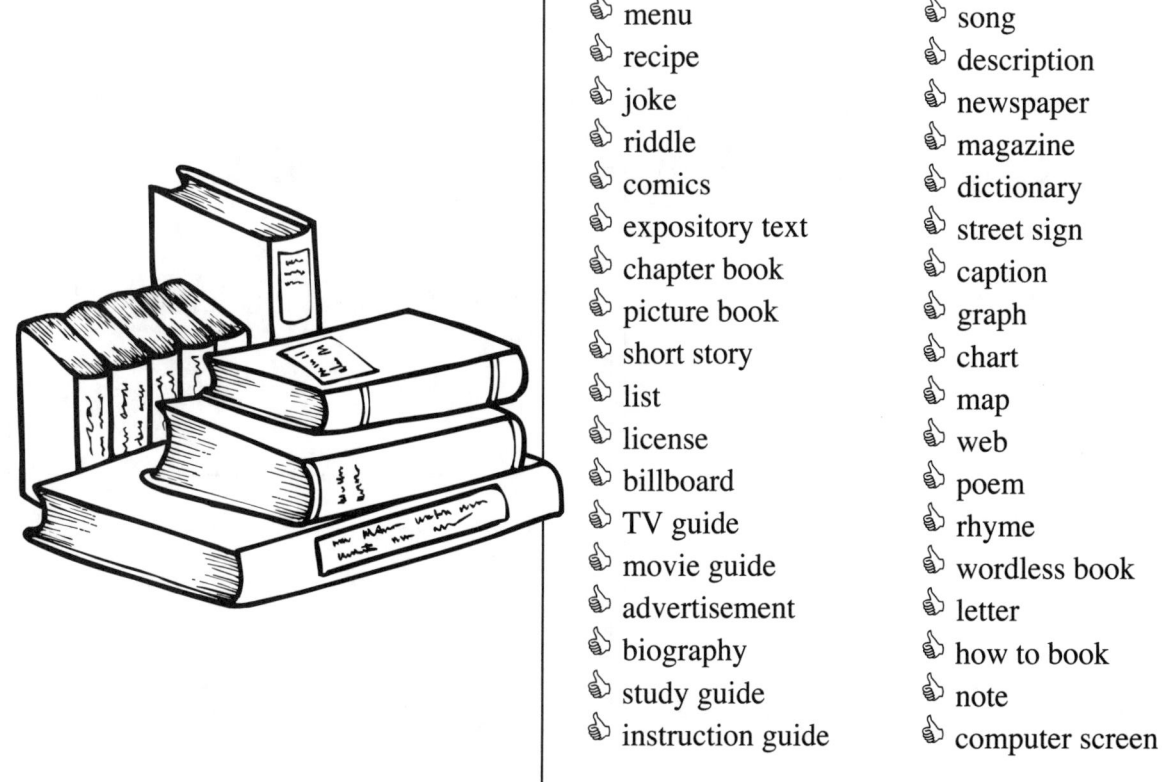

- 👍 menu
- 👍 recipe
- 👍 joke
- 👍 riddle
- 👍 comics
- 👍 expository text
- 👍 chapter book
- 👍 picture book
- 👍 short story
- 👍 list
- 👍 license
- 👍 billboard
- 👍 TV guide
- 👍 movie guide
- 👍 advertisement
- 👍 biography
- 👍 study guide
- 👍 instruction guide
- 👍 song
- 👍 description
- 👍 newspaper
- 👍 magazine
- 👍 dictionary
- 👍 street sign
- 👍 caption
- 👍 graph
- 👍 chart
- 👍 map
- 👍 web
- 👍 poem
- 👍 rhyme
- 👍 wordless book
- 👍 letter
- 👍 how to book
- 👍 note
- 👍 computer screen

Creating a Classroom Library

Designing

Selecting

Organizing

Labeling

Books should be labeled

by how they

_____

rather than

_____

they represent

Classroom Libraries

Why: Unquestionably, self-selected independent reading is a high priority classroom goal. In *The Power of Reading* (1993), Stephen Krashen expertly cites research to highlight the critical nature of daily meaningful engagement in authentic literacy experiences. Classroom libraries provide an excellent way to promote these experiences and should be a part of every classroom across grade levels. Placing time and energy on making valuable resources accessible says loudly, *I place a high value on reading and want you to have many opportunities to spend quality time with good books!* The classroom library provides a way to organize choices, and is most effectively utilized when the school day is structured so that an emphasis is placed on providing multiple exposure to pleasurable reading in dedicated blocks of time. If children are to become avid readers, the adults in their lives must make pleasurable reading the ultimate goal. This means respecting student choices by viewing independent reading as a child controlled activity. The perfect definition of independent reading should serve as a constant reminder: *Butt out!*

Where: The location of the classroom library is an important consideration. Designate an area away from noise and movement where children can curl up with a good book alone or with a buddy. While space constraints may limit the options available, pillows, plants and books galore will aid in this process. When space is limited, two book cases can be pushed together in an L-shape to block off a small area. The size of the library area is far less important than how inviting it is. Engage students in designing the library and making these decisions so that they will take ownership of it. This may include student advertisements, book recommendations and enticing signs that say loud and clear, *Come in, relax, and read...read...read!*

What: Most importantly, the contents of the classroom library should reflect student interests and reading level over their grade level designation. This means finding worthy texts and engaging students in the process of selecting and organizing these resources. Because the library will be used for self-selected reading, at least ten to fifteen books should be available at each child's *independent* reading level. Variety is important, so include expository and narrative, chapter books, picture books, poetry, newspapers, magazines, joke books and comic books in unlimited quantities. Texts should be organized in some way such as in plastic tubs to provide easy access. Research also shows that readers are more likely to select books when the cover is facing forward. Jim Trelease suggests using rain gutters for this purpose. The library should be brimming with texts that reflect student interests. The more choices that are available, the more apt students are to use the library. These efforts will pay off handsomely as children begin to *choose* to read for real purposes, having many opportunities to do so on a daily basis.

Organizing Texts for Independent Reading

Piece Of Cake

- Not much print
- One or three lines
- Larger letter size
- Pictures on every page
- Interesting topic
- Personal knowledge
- Know vocabulary
- Comfortable to read
- Easy to understand

Take It Easy

- Quite a bit of print
- Four to six lines
- A little bigger print
- Pictures on most pages
- Interesting topic
- Some Knowledge
- A few hard words
- A little uncomfortable
- Understand most

Whoa!

- Full pages of print
- More than six lines
- Small letter size
- Very few pictures
- Uninteresting topic
- Little knowledge
- Many hard words
- Very uncomfortable
- Hard to understand

Invitations to Reading

Book Blessings	Personality Reading
A _____ advertisement to highlight _____ texts	A _____ advertisement to highlight _____ texts
	When	
	What	
	How	

Strategy-at-a-Glance

Strategy: *Book Blessings* (Linda Gambrell)

Description: A daily strategy for recommending teacher-selected texts for independent reading purposes, using a brief overview of varied texts to entice readers.

Step-By-Step:
1. There is an old saying that what one does speaks louder than what one says. This is particularly true when it comes to associating value with reading. It is impossible to demonstrate that a high value is placed on these experiences when opportunities are not forthcoming. Conversely, exhibiting immense enthusiasm for books and guaranteeing quality time to spend with them says, *I care deeply about this wonderful thing called reading.* Time set aside for children to savor a good book is never wasted and should be a daily goal, balancing the school day with both instruction (*how*) and opportunity (*why*). This message *does* speak louder than words, and the long range implications are far-reaching. An important aspect of creating more motivated readers is to designate dedicated blocks of time for children to spend with good books while making a variety of books accessible for these purposes. Daily book blessings provide an easy way to do this.

2. Book Blessings allow the teacher to expose children to specific titles throughout the year. Select at least ten books to "bless" each week. Books may be blessed on Monday and made available through the week, or several books may be blessed daily. Careful consideration should go into book selections, focusing on independent reading level rather than grade level. There should be great variety in genre, difficulty, and format, including books, magazines, articles, joke books, comics and poetry. Consider the range represented by students so there is something for everyone each week.

3. Every morning, the teacher "blesses" books by giving an overview (*The first book I have is called <u>Exploring Africa</u>. The beautiful pictures of animals will make you feel like you are on an African Safari. The next book is called <u>Butterflies</u>. If you are interested in how grasshoppers turn into butterflies, you will love this book. <u>Silly Rabbits</u> is a funny story about a family of rabbits who do some very silly things. It will make you laugh out loud.*). Show the cover of each book and one or two key pages, drawing attention to any features that may build anticipation and enthusiasm. It is suggested at least one book each week comes with a taped version to offer variety and options and provide a support system.

4. Once books have been blessed, place them in a visible area such as the classroom library where they are available for self-selected, independent reading throughout the day. These are featured books, so they should be arranged in a prominent place with the cover showing.

5. To extend book blessings, individual children may volunteer to "bless" a personal reading. This provides an advertisement while students benefit from the sharing process.

Strategy-at-a-Glance

Strategy: *Personality Reading*

Description: A meaningful way for students to revisit a self-selected personal reading by sharing key points to celebrate and advertise favorite books.

Step-By-Step:

1. Personality reading is an outstanding way to give students responsibility for highlighting and sharing a personal reading. Valuable learning occurs through revisiting and condensing a text for sharing purposes while the sharing is an opportunity to promote interest for others. The child self-selects a familiar book and prepares before sharing. Sharing takes only a few minutes, allowing several children to participate each morning, so that one-to-one support can be offered as appropriate. The optional form provided will allow students to think this through on paper and include an illustration to support the sharing process.

2. **Overview**: The child begins by giving a brief overview of the book, generally one or two sentences to summarize key ideas. This includes the title, author and brief book talk (*My book is about _____*). Remind the child not to give away too much. The overview should give readers an idea what the story is about while stimulating interest in reading through inviting language (*This is a really funny book about _____.; This exciting story will put you on the edge of your seat and make your heart pound.*). A tremendous amount of learning occurs as children consider the essence of the reading by selecting key points to condense it for sharing purposes. This makes it time well spent.

3. **Hook**: The child now prepares listeners for the reading that will follow (*I'm going to read the part where _____.*). This combines with the overview to "hook" readers and prepare them for the sample, providing one more way to build anticipation.

4. **The Sample**: The child now reads aloud a brief selection, generally not to exceed thirty to sixty seconds of text. The sample should exemplify what the story is about and what makes the book worth reading. It is always selected by the child, providing a good reason for repeated practice, which ensures smooth, accurate reading with expression and enthusiasm. Repeated exposure to a specific section of print serves to build fluency, comprehension and confidence as well as to reinforce sight vocabulary.

5. After Personality Readings are completed each morning, provide time for peers to ask questions about the books. Questions may relate to length, use of pictures and any information that will help readers decide if it is for them. This is brief as books will be displayed for a closer look after sharing.

6. A sign labeled *Our Personality Books for Today* can be created so that books presented each morning are displayed on the top shelf of the library with the cover facing forward. This places books in clear view so they are easily accessible to interested readers.

My Personality Reading Sharing Form

The book I have selected is

_____

It is written by

_____

I think this book is worth reading because

_____
_____
_____

I will summarize the story in this way

_____
_____
_____
_____

I selected the sample on page _____ because

_____
_____
_____

©2004 by Dr. Mary Howard

My Personality Reading Sharing Form

I am going to share this picture

I will introduce my picture in this way
_____
_____
_____
_____

This is a good picture to share my book because
_____
_____
_____

©2004 by Dr. Mary Howard

Reflective Pause #1

Do you provide dedicated blocks of time for children to read meaningful texts for real purposes?

Reinforced Current learning	Stimulated New learning

Critical Consideration #2

Build _____ experiences into the day.

Assessing Fluency

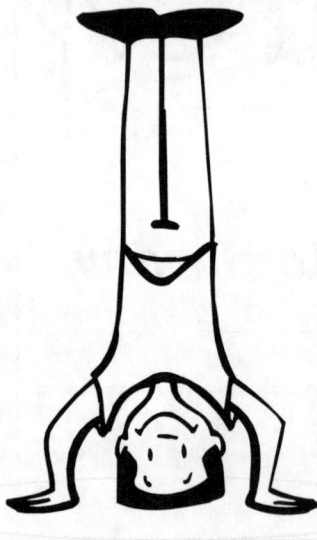

Words Per Minute

Words	oral reading	silent reading
Pre Primer	13-35 wpm	
Primer	28-68 wpm	
Grade 1	31-67 wpm	
Grade 2	52-102 wpm	58-122 wpm
Grade 3	85-139 wpm	96-168 wpm
Grade 4	78-124 wpm	107-175 wpm
Grade 6	113-165 wpm	135-241 wpm

Leslie & Caldwell (2001)

Criteria

• Does the reading resemble language to *sound like someone is talking*?

• Is the reading smooth and with a minimum of hesitations and repetitions?

• Is the pace of reading adapted in appropriate places to fit the story?

• Is vocal expression evident so that it matches and enhances the meaning?

• Are punctuation signals observed and read by stopping or pausing at appropriate places?

• Are words grouped into meaningful phrases?

Classroom Contexts for Building Fluency

- Rhyming texts
- Alphabet books
- Rhythmic language
- Alliteration
- Tongue twisters
- Nursery rhymes
- Songs
- Rap
- Poetry
- Playful language
- Reader's Theater
- Dialogue
- Repeated Reading
- Taped Practice
- Demonstrations

 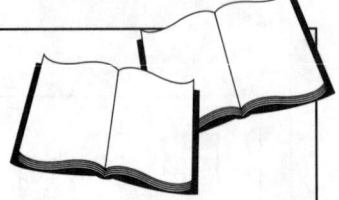

Poetry Quilt

Poetry is an outstanding source for oral reading, providing immediate access to a wide range of varied and interesting selections. Brief texts make it easy to secure multiple copies at a variety of instructional levels and provide a wonderful resource for struggling readers in many ways:

unlimited sources

tremendous variety

brief texts

non grade specific (no "baby" poems)

cross-curricular subjects

natural source for fluency

rich language

high level vocabulary

rhythmic element

pleasurable mode for reading

A *Poetry Quilt* can be created to display poems organized by category. Sew pockets onto a piece of quilted material, with a strip of lace stitched around the border for decoration. Pockets can be labeled with categories as shown below, with a second set of smaller pockets to house instrumental music to accompany readings. Full page copies of favorite poems can be duplicated, using smaller cardstock versions for quilt pockets.

 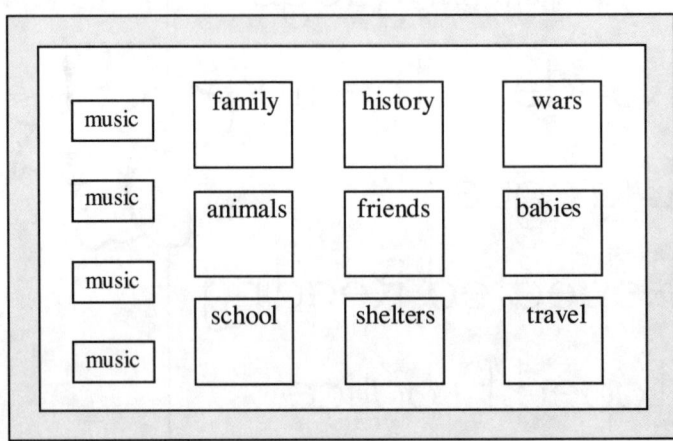

Use the full page blackline masters to create *Personal Poetry Books*. This is a collection of each child's favorite poems with personalized illustrations that will provide another excellent source for fluency practice. Children may also revisit poems with a partner through self-selected activities, such as identifying interesting or unusual words, comparing/contrasting related poems or creating a pool of rhyming words.

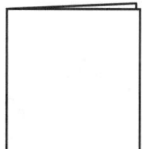 # Personal Friendly Folder

A friendly folder is a collection of personal texts that a child is able to read independently with fluency and comprehension. Texts are always self-selected for silent reading practice and oral reading fluency so both motivation and engagement are high. Friendly Folders make it easy for children to practice alone or with a buddy. At least ten minutes a day for rereading is optimal to provide several benefits:

> to build *confidence*
>
> to increase *fluency*
>
> to *practice* good strategies

Although students will self-select texts for inclusion in the folder, the teacher may suggest potential sources *(You read this like someone is talking. This might be a good choice for your Friendly Folder).* It is recommended that at least five to ten selections remain in the folder at all times to provide choice and variety, removing and replacing texts throughout the year as appropriate. Selections may include:

Possible Contents

- letters
- notes
- journals
- stories
- newspaper
- magazine
- songs
- rhymes
- poems
- dictated writing
- recipes
- riddles

Friendly Reminders (written on the inside cover)

 I am interested in reading it

 I can read it by myself.

 I can read it like someone is talking.

 I understand what I am reading.

Transparency Story

Step By Step
1.
2.
3.
4.
5.

What?
High _____
_____ reading experiences

How?
Slightly familiar
Brief texts
Manageable chunks

Strategy-at-a-Glance

Strategy: *Transparency Story*

Description: A meaningful format for revisiting classroom favorites for repeated reading as a group or with a buddy through an enlarged personalized version.

Step-By-Step:

1. Transparency story is an excellent way to create enlarged story samples for instructional and informal reading purposes, particularly when multiple copies are not available. Stories provide repeated practice, so be sure enthusiasm is high for rereading. Brief texts such as poetry, songs or short stories (expository and narrative) are ideal. It is suggested that children are exposed to the text first to provide familiarity with the language.

2. Record each page of text on blank sheets and overheads, and distribute them to individual children or a small group so they can be illustrated alone or collaboratively. In this way, each child is responsible only for a small section of text. Initial drawings are completed on plain paper or the optional form provided and transferred to the transparency later. This makes it easy for children to modify the drawing before placing it in the final form on the transparency. Encourage children to create an illustration that matches the print as closely as possible.

3. As children complete drawings, the teacher rotates to draw attention to the print (*Why are there three monsters? Where does it say three?*). Continuously make connections between the drawing and the print by encouraging children to analyze both (*You said the monster is licking the painting. How could you make this more obvious in your picture?*), engaging them in modifying it as applicable (*I could add a tongue.*) and reinforcing any changes (*Good idea. That would match the words and make it easier for me to see it in your drawing.*). This provides an excellent opportunity to highlight key words and use the picture to build meaning.

4. Once the drawing has been modified, it can now be transferred to the transparency that has been prepared for each page. This is easily done by placing the original behind the transparency and tracing the completed drawing with permanent color markers.

5. When drawings are completed, provide time for students to practice their page alone or with a buddy. This will provide repeated practice and exposure to the print while keeping the focus on fluency and accuracy. Each child will share their page in sequence, reading the print orally and verbalizing why specific choices were made in the drawing, pointing to words as appropriate (*I made a flower painting because it says it right here.*). This verbalization provides a model for the reading as well as the thinking involved in generating drawings.

6. After sharing, number the pages and place them in a folder with the title and author written on the front. The text is now ready to be used as a shared or choral reading activity, for independent reading or as a buddy reading literacy center. Vocabulary cards may also be created to reinforce the print and provide an opportunity for extension.

Transparency Story Planning Form

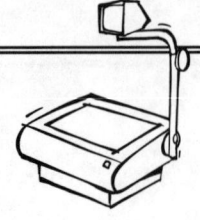

This is the part of the story I am going to picture

(circle all the words that are important)

These are important words to include in my picture

_____ _____ _____

_____ _____ _____

I will include these ideas in my picture

- _____
- _____
- _____
- _____
- _____

©2004 by Dr. Mary Howard

(Draw your picture in the space below)

I changed _____

I added _____

I am proud of _____

©2004 by Dr. Mary Howard

FOOT BOOK

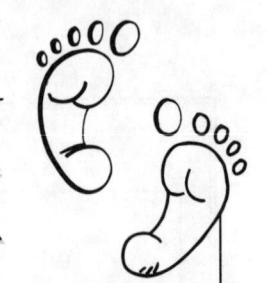

| 1 |
| 2 |
| 3 |
| 4 |
| 5 |

Step By Step

Sources

Poetry

Songs

Rhymes

Nursery rhymes

Rhythmic texts

Picture book

Alphabet books

Raps

Strategy-at-a-Glance

Strategy: *Foot Books*

Description: A repeated reading strategy incorporating movement by allowing children to walk on print while reading, pointing to words with alternate feet.

Step-By-Step:

1. A Foot Book is easy to create. It should be a brief text, generally ten to fifteen pages for the completed product. This makes poetry, songs, raps, short picture books and nursery rhymes a perfect source. Movement makes any rhythmic texts particularly effective.

2. Begin by dividing the selection into individual pages. *Humpty Dumpty*, for example, may include four pages:

        Page 1: Humpty Dumpty sat on a wall.
        Page 2: Humpty Dumpty had a great fall.
        Page 3: All the king's horses and all the king's men
        Page 4: Couldn't put Humpty together again.

3. Write each section of text on cardstock cards, generally 8 1/2 by 11 inches, to make the book sturdy enough to walk on. A footprint is glued to the opposite side of each page, making sure the text and footprints alternate from the right to left side of the card.

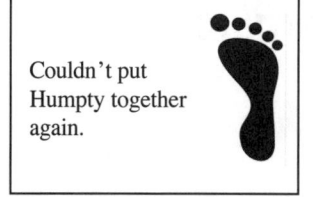

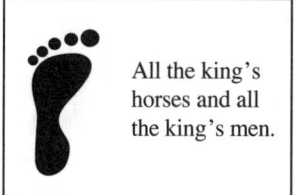

4. Student volunteers can illustrate the pages, adding a picture above or below the print. Matching the text with a visual will encourage careful reading and close observation. The personalized illustrations and bright colors will make Foot Books a classroom favorite.

5. Combine the pages as shown, making the text move in a forward progression as it is read from bottom to top. Laminate cards first to prolong the life of the books, adding tape to the back of each card for strength and durability. Be sure to leave a slight gap between pages so that they can be folded in accordion style for easy storage. Favorite texts, songs and poems can gradually be added and stored in a decorated box to use and reuse. Books can also be used for home practice.

6. The Foot Book is now ready for students to *walk and read*. They simply place the appropriate foot on the footprint and point to the words with the toes of the opposite foot. This is an excellent independent reading activity, particularly for students needing movement. It can also be used as a buddy reading activity as students take turns reading and checking.

Reflective Pause #2

Do you offer experiences for self-selected repeated reading to build fluency and meaning?

Reinforced Current learning	Stimulated New learning

Critical Consideration #3

Build _____ and _____ .

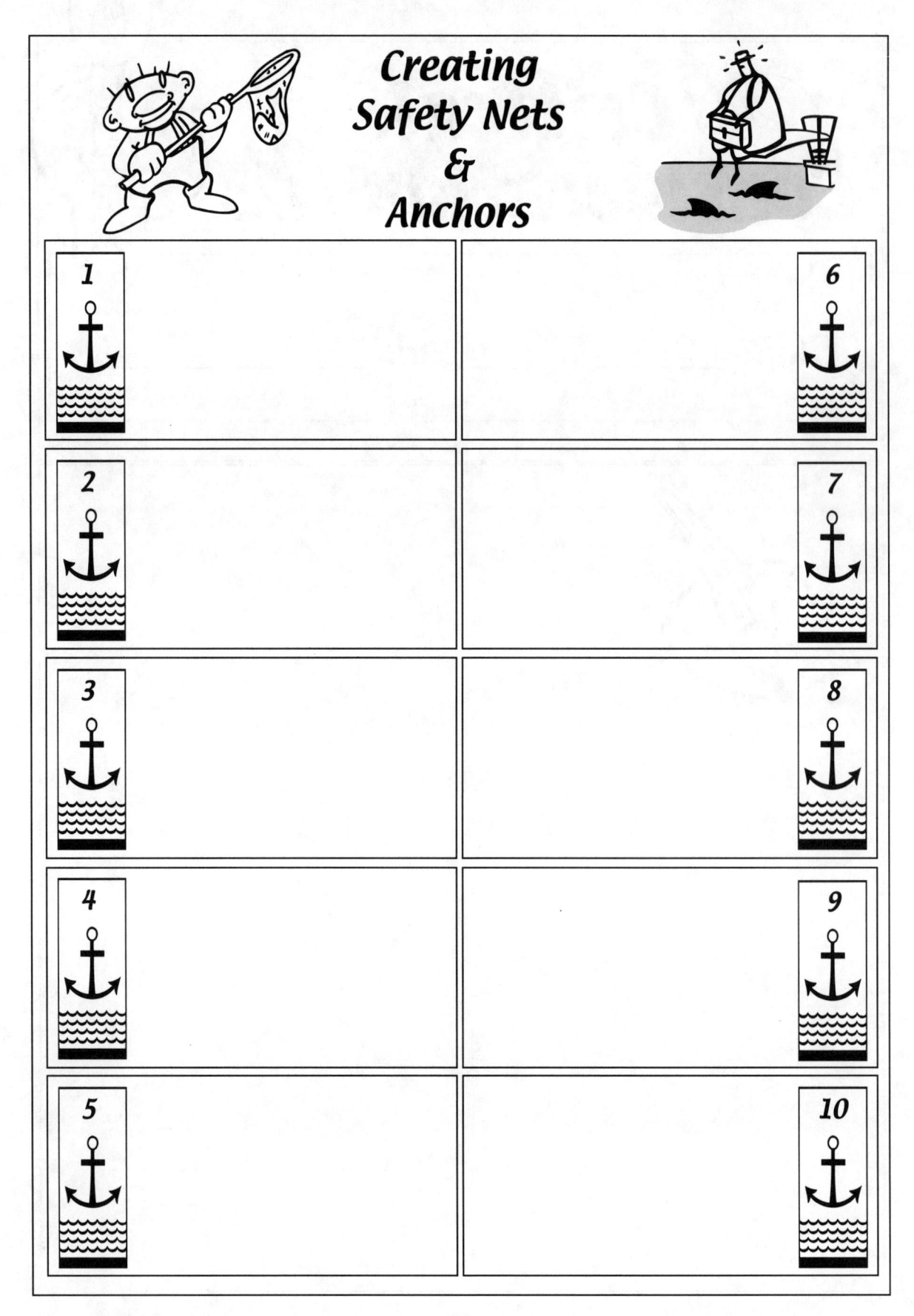

Creating Safety Nets & Anchors

1	**6**
2	**7**
3	**8**
4	**9**
5	**10**

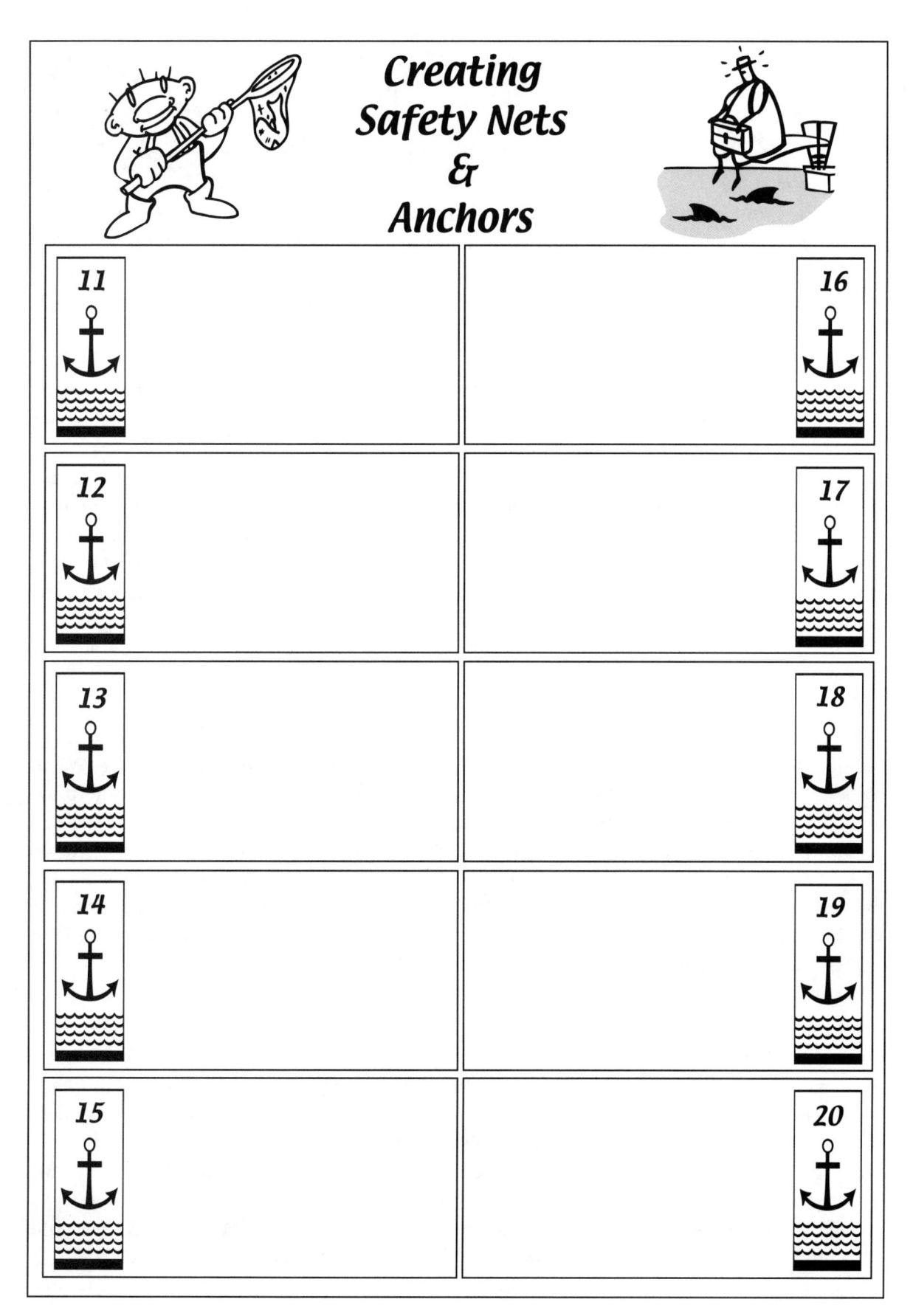

Creating Safety Nets & Anchors

11		16	
12		17	
13		18	
14		19	
15		20	

Safety Nets & Anchors

Success should be a guarantee in *every* classroom for *every* child *without exception*. First, this means alleviating frustrating and overwhelming tasks, particularly for struggling readers who often view school as synonymous with failure. Secondly, this means finding, celebrating and building on existing strengths. Several easy-to-implement strategies will provide a starting point for turning this guarantee into a promise.

Model learning daily: The ultimate goal of teaching is for learning to transfer to other contexts and become habituated. But teaching does not guarantee that this will happen unless *process* is rooted in each learning task. Referred to as *metacognition*, process is evident when children can verbalize the thinking that led to a task. Some children have a strong foundation for the learning and so are constantly making connections from known to new. For many struggling readers, however, this thinking is more complicated because they are missing rich and varied experiences that lay the groundwork for new learning. Through teacher models such as think-aloud and demonstrations on a daily basis, the thinking process is made public. Responsibility is then gradually relinquished to students so that instruction can respond directly to the successes and confusions children are acknowledging and verbalizing.

Begin with the Big Picture: Good readers use a wide range of information before reading, building anticipation and setting a purpose to guide meaning throughout the reading. When readers take advantage of the author's clues, these clues can serve to activate prior knowledge and experiences that engage children in purposeful reading. Strategies such as previewing the cover and illustrations, reading the first or last paragraph or using the table of contents combine to provide a *direction* while making students more responsible for meaning-making after reading. A supportive introduction or overview and questions or graphic organizers initiated *before* reading provide a clear purpose, stimulate thinking *during* reading and support revisiting the text *after* reading.

Explore varied learning contexts: Research tells us that new learning must be presented a minimum of three to ten times in varied contexts to become permanent. Unfortunately, teachers feel so compelled to *cover* the curriculum that there are few opportunities to *linger a bit longer*. These multiple contexts are particularly important for struggling readers because they may have limited exposure outside the school setting. Strategies may include varying the way information is presented, reading related texts, providing alternative forms such as graphic organizers or multi-media resources, presenting information in unique ways such as a rap or song, or translating learning in a new format such as Reader's Theater. With each repetition in a new context, the *threads* of learning are gradually being connected.

Address multiple pathways: Redundancy, an important component of learning, occurs when more than one pathway is activated. When multiple sensory systems are addressed through a variety of instructional strategies, *back-up systems* for learning are provided. The more back up systems in place, the greater the likelihood that appropriate pathways have been activated for that child. Teaching to different modalities (tactile-kinesthetic, visual and auditory) or emphasizing the brain-body connection through movement provides these alternative pathways as well as repetition. In other words, the way (or number of ways) information is presented is as important as the information itself. This makes instructional variety and flexibility the key, acknowledging that there are *many ways of knowing*.

Extend time frames: Providing extra time struggling learners need is complicated in today's busy classrooms, but it is essential for supplying additional opportunities to process learning or for offering support in the initial stages. This is particularly true when other challenges compete for attention such as spelling, memory or language. Students may start a task that morning or the day before, listen to a taped version before discussion, watch a video or begin with a study guide or summary. Small instructional groups may be formed so a mini-lesson can set the stage for the learning that will follow. This allows the teacher to build important concepts on a one-to-one basis, equaling the playing field just a bit and providing a starting point before meeting in a whole group setting. This allows the teacher to create successful experiences by addressing individual needs in small group contexts first. (Note: Remember that time is irrelevant if the task is not appropriate in the first place).

Implement auditory supports: Many struggling readers have difficulty learning through strictly auditory channels, often due to attention issues or language delays. A variety of auditory supports can become powerful strategies to accommodate for these variations. This may include repeating learning or reading for *the second chance group* or providing a tape recorded version of information so that children can revisit it for a second, third or fourth listening as appropriate. This may be a teacher recording or students can create their own to provide a scaffold when the task is challenging. For example, children who struggle with writing may tape record a personal piece in progress. The recording can then be used in the editing process so the focus is on meaning over mechanics.

Increase repetition and practice: Every time children practice new learning, that learning is being strengthened by reinforcing what children already know at an easy level. This is particularly important if practice is not offered outside the school setting or when frustration level tasks make practice irrelevant. Repetition and practice *over time* make the difference, keeping in mind that repetition makes *permanent*, not perfect. This means that continued monitoring during the practice stage is important. Reinforcement activities include repeated reading for fluency and meaning and revisiting new learning through easy and slightly challenging independent and collaborative activities such as literacy centers and meaningful seatwork activities. As long as these experiences are valuable and purposeful and designed to reinforce rather than teach, this is time well spent. Homework falls in this category.

Present learning in smaller chunks: A theme present in each safety net is the detrimental effect of teaching too much. This is the result of increasing demands on memory and diminished time to practice. Children learn less as teachers teach more, making *Teach Less Better* a powerful guide for instruction. In 1956, George Miller found that the average adult was able to hold only seven (plus or minus two) chunks of information at one time. *Chunking*, or the ability to hold more in memory when it is presented in manageable chunks, increases the potential for remembering. Less information provides more opportunities for connecting known to new and for practicing new learning. This can be applied to reading as well, stopping periodically at key points to reflect, connect, and dissect meaning-making in progress while teaching *on the run*. Trimming down the curriculum means alleviating trivial information (and activities) so that more time is available for the things that really matter.

Probe for understanding: The text is a rich and valuable resource, too often neglected, that provides wonderful examples and details that will support ideas. This should be an important focus of teaching, providing many opportunities for students to revisit the text in meaningful ways. The teacher's role is to reinforce current knowledge and teach new learning with a *gentle nudge* that encourages more thoughtful reading (*Tell me more.; Give me an example.; Where did you see that?; Show me.; Prove it.*). This holds students accountable for supporting ideas while their responses can inform teaching and provide rich opportunities to extend learning in a variety of ways. Use the text as a valuable resource throughout reading, drawing attention to key points and encouraging children to justify thinking.

Encourage personal transformation: Simply spitting back answers to questions, or *regurgitating* learning, does not demonstrate understanding. Learning is evident when children can *transform* what has been learned by combining the text with personal experiences and putting it into their own words. Provide students with many opportunities for transformation. Students may restate and translate their learning, using examples from the text or from their own lives as a means to modify and elaborate on definitions, retellings, and summaries. Self-questioning is an important form of transformation, and encouraging students to pose thoughtful questions will stimulate meaning.

Make language the bridge: Reading, a relatively new invention, is not natural to the human brain. Language, however, is a natural and inborn human ability that can build a bridge to this difficult task. Providing information orally before children are asked to read or listen creates a link between oral and written language. This can be critical for children who struggle with print. Oral rehearsals, or orally summarizing and restating what will follow, will build a support before reading. During and after reading, encourage students to reflect orally (*Turn to a neighbor and tell them one thing you have learned about sea turtles.*) or summarize what they have read. These opportunities to hook the meaning of the print through oral language are powerful frames for learning. Read-aloud is an excellent model, using oral reading as a springboard to print.

Integrate memory aids: Much of school learning falls into the category of semantic (factual) knowledge. Examples are weekly spelling tests or memorizing the name of the presidents. Semantic memory is the least effective system, requiring a great deal of repetition and a relatively good memory. This is a complicating factor for struggling readers, particularly for tasks that increase the demand on memory such as writing and discussion after reading. This is increasingly problematic for longer chapter books or units over time. Unfortunately, recall is often confused with comprehension. Avoid trivial recall questions for children who struggle with memory *(What was the character's name? What date did it occur?).* Build in memory supports such as sticky notes, key words, quick draws or oral and written summaries. In short, teach children *how* to remember, making sure what you are asking them to remember is worth holding on to.

Offer alternate response modes: In many classrooms, children are told how and what to learn and given few choices in the process. This philosophy of educational control fails to respect that different strategies are more effective for some children than others. There are many varied ways to accomplish the same end goals, making choice and option important. Rather than demanding a literature response, several alternatives may be suggested so that children can select the one most appropriate. This also increases confidence and motivation by giving children a sense of control over the learning process. Students may, for example, elect to draw rather than write about learning, read orally on a tape recorder rather than present it to peers, or create a mind map or graphic organizer rather than an outline. Alternatives and choices acknowledge that there are many effective paths that lead to learning, while helping children explore their own unique way of thinking.

Include social collaboration: Learning should never be a lonely, solitary activity. The more collaboration children are offered in respectful and non threatening environments, the greater the potential for learning. Rather than segregating students on the basis of achievement, social learning allows them to become teacher and learner in this process. Provide varied modes for meaningfully collaborating with peers such as sharing with a partner or small group. These contexts celebrate what *every* child brings to the table so that each child is seen as a valuable and contributing member of the school community. This spirit of collaboration should be a part of every day.

Build in reflective pauses: Research tells us that the average teacher offers three to five seconds of wait time before calling on a child or providing the answer. Struggling readers need extra time to reflect and process before responding. If the answer is always given by others before the child can even formulate it, the extra effort is hardly worth the trouble. This often results in negative behaviors such as withdrawal or acting out. A minimum of seven to ten seconds provides time to *chew it up and spit it out* before responding. Create rituals such as reflecting silently before raising hands, writing key words on an index card or circling the response on a list of choices. These activities will give children who need it time to reflect while making responses more "thoughtful" in nature.

Provide elaborated feedback: There is no question that feedback is an important component of learning. Yet, it is often too late, too trivial and too passive. *That's right...that's wrong* does little to teach children what to do differently in the future. Effective feedback is immediate and specific and it engages learners by making them accountable for the process over the product. Elaborated feedback gives students an active role (*Were you right?; Prove it!*) while reinforcing thinking (*I like what you did here. What were you thinking?*) and prompting new learning (*Think about this.; Read this again.; Did you notice_____?; Remember when ____*), so it is more likely to transfer to other contexts.

Use visual hooks: Auditory modes are challenging at best for many struggling readers, while visual processing systems are often strong. Visual hooks such as pictures, posters, charts, webs, graphs, graphic organizers, drawings or other visual representations provide a strong mode for remembering before, during and after learning. Teach children to create personal visuals for learning (*Put that in picture form*) such as a quick sketch, web or graph. These visual anchors will support and enhance meaning throughout reading and provide scaffolds for discussion or writing activities that follow.

Highlight dramatic engagement: Drama is an important pathway to learning because it engages the entire body and creates emotional connections. Give learning a dramatic twist through expressive oral readings or dramatic interpretations. These activities maximize learning because the emotional impact, movement and fluency that accompanies them engages the child in a variety of ways, making learning more *memorable*. This is particularly important for children who are often disconnected from learning or who learn best through a tactile-kinesthetic (movement) mode. Engage students in writing their own scripts to act out or in selecting the source for oral reading for a more active role.

Create text scaffolds: Text scaffolds can be a critical factor for enhancing understanding. Yet, these often go untapped by failing to make these support systems explicit. Text scaffolds include the table of contents, typographical features such as bold, highlighted, bulleted or underlined print, first and/or last paragraphs, illustrations, captions, and graphs. These aids can provide ongoing support systems for meaning-making throughout reading. Student scaffolds may include rewriting subheadings into question form, summarizing key ideas orally and in writing, or using a study guide or outline to support learning.

Emphasize "life" strategies: School success is a meager goal that is generally far removed from the real world. Focus on teaching strategies to build on existing strengths and strategies that compensate for areas of weakness. Successful adults have learned to *self medicate* by finding a quiet place when attention wanes or creating personal organizational systems. Allowing children to stand during reading, use sticky notes as memory aids, hold onto a koosh ball for movement, or create personal structures for organization will develop these "life" strategies. Success in life becomes more relevant than success in school as we begin to acknowledge that uniqueness is what makes the most successful adults successful.

I can implement these safety nets & anchors...

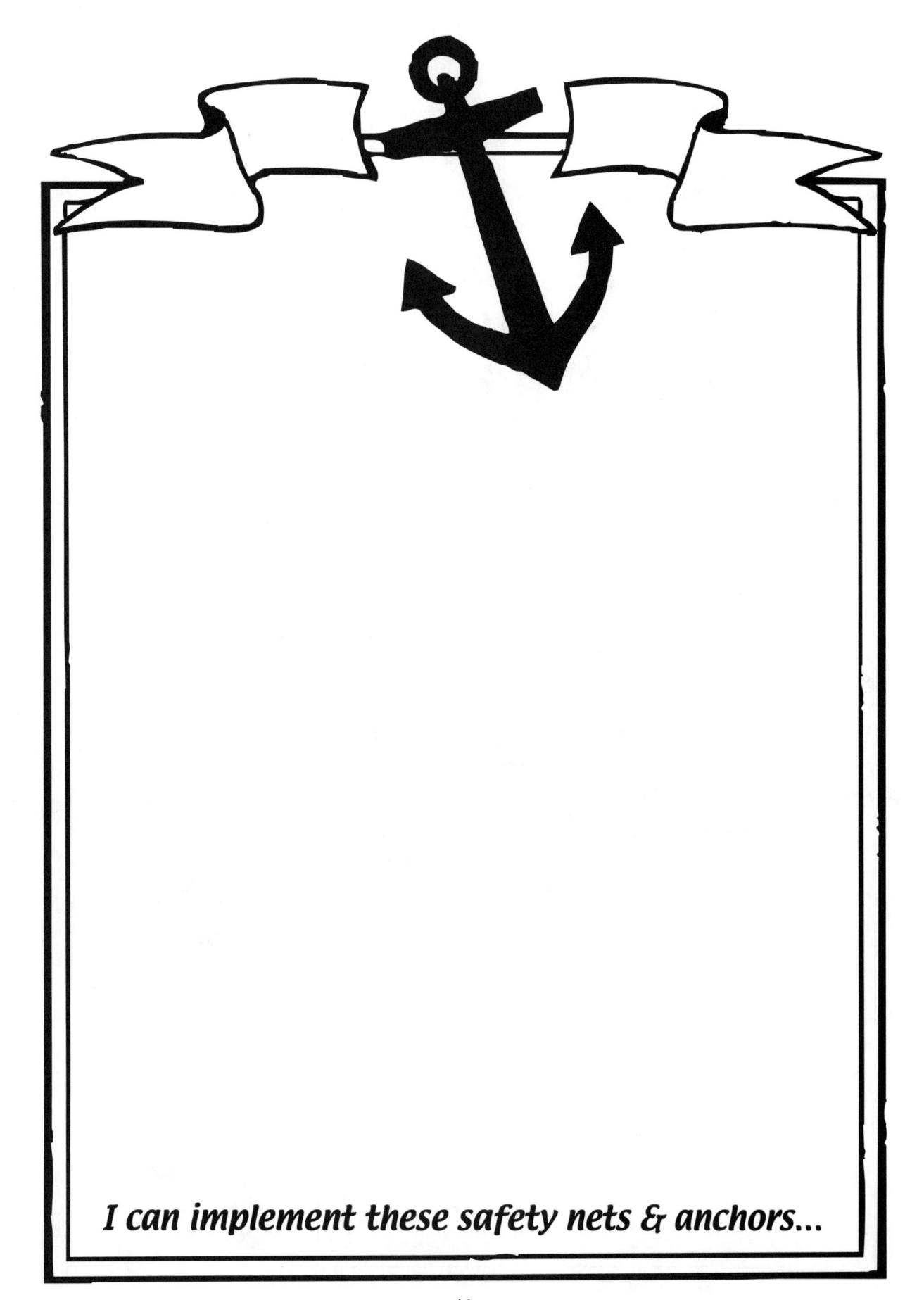

THE VISUAL HOOK

Poster
Chart
Diagram
Photograph
Picture
Cartoon
Map
Caption
Web
Organizer
Mind map
Study guide
Drawing

What Hooks Do you Offer?

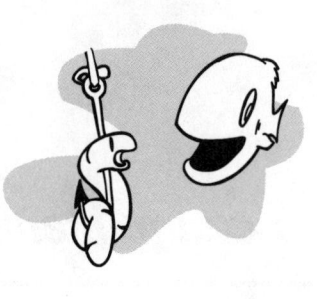

Worksheets.. Neurological Dead End Streets

When selected cautiously on a limited basis for the right purposes, worksheets can be an effective tool to reinforce what children have learned. In many classrooms, however, worksheets sadly serve as a substitute for authentic literacy experiences. This results in passive learning as the teacher relinquishes responsibility to the publisher. Worksheets rarely contribute to new learning and generally focus on a "skill and drill" mentality. Tate aptly described these drawbacks with her title phrase, *Worksheets Don't Grow Dendrites* (2003), in which she emphasizes the questionable practice of trivial paper-pencil (or computerized) tasks that focus on isolated skills over real learning events.

Several problems associated with worksheets are compounded for struggling readers. Children needing movement and active engagement must sit passively at a desk. Children already disconnected from learning participate in boring and trivial tasks. Children needing massive doses of authentic application and practice are forced to focus on isolated skills. Children needing the *process* participate in tasks that emphasize the product. Children who struggle most getting thoughts on paper are given activities that focus heavily on paper-pencil tasks. Children finding multiple step directions difficult must weed through written instructions that are often confusing and vague. Children who thrive on social interaction have few opportunities for collaboration. Children needing reflective feedback most are given little more than low level substitutions.

Two questions always seem to arise: *What is the alternative?* and *Where do grades come from?* These questions are based on the flawed assumption that worksheets are a good source for learning *or* grading in the first place. Sitting passively at a desk completing meaningless activities with little or no support is impossible to justify, particularly for children who don't have a minute to spare. These students need active participation in meaningful literacy activities that include variety, multiple modalities, social interaction and active engagement. Further, worksheets should never be used for grading purposes as they are designed to reinforce at an easy level. The alternative, much simpler than it may seem, is to select worthwhile and meaningful activities, identify the end goal and establish grading criteria based on these goals. This can be effectively done by creating rubrics, or a list of descriptors that will be used to determine grades. While this may take more time, it is always worthwhile if the goal is to provide valuable learning experiences that have the power to inform teaching. Most importantly, time is not wasted for the children who can least afford it. Never delude yourself into thinking that passive activities enhance learning in any way.

Reflective Pause #3

Do you consider current learning needs, building scaffolds to guarantee success for every child?

Reinforced Current learning	Stimulated New learning

Critical Consideration #4

Select _____ texts & tasks.

Balancing Text Needs

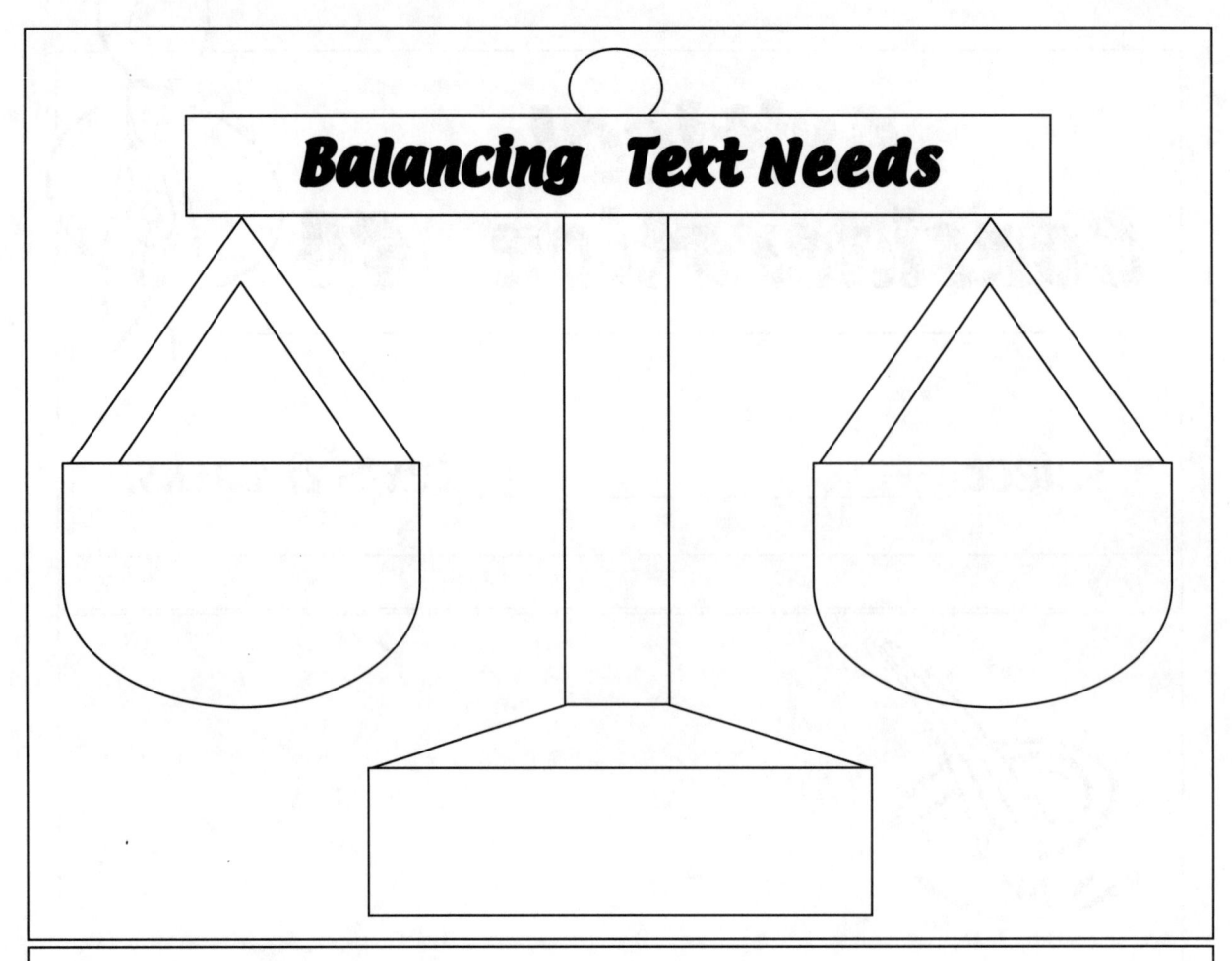

Question	independent	instructional	frustration
How Much			
How Often			
Why			

On My Own Reading

- Have you read this book many times before?
- Do you know almost all the words?
- Do you understand it very well?
- Can you read it fairly quickly and smoothly?
- Do you use expression when you read?
- Can you easily tell someone about what you read?
- Can you read this book without anyone to help you?
- Do you feel very confident as you read?
- Are you very interested in this topic?

With Support Reading

- Is this a new or almost new book for you?
- Do you know most of the words on each page?
- Do you understand most of what you are reading?
- Are there some parts you have to read slowly?
- Do you read some parts fairly smoothly and quickly?
- Do you use some expression as you read?
- Is there someone who can help you when you need it?
- Can you tell someone about most of what you've read?
- Is the topic interesting to you?

Ear Reading

- Is this a new book for you?
- Are there many words on each page you don't know?
- Is it hard to understand what you read?
- Do you read slowly word-by-word?
- Do you have to struggle on every page?
- Do you feel uncomfortable as you read?
- Is it difficult to explain what you've read?
- Do you have to work out the hard parts on your own?
- Is this topic boring to you?

Adapted from *The Goldilocks Strategy* by Ohlhausen & Jepsen, 1992

My Personal Selections	On My Own	With Support	Ear Reading

©2004 by Dr. Mary Howard

Stretch a sentence

Getting Started

Identify a key idea in the form of a brief sentence that will serve to provide an _____ of the story, activate _____ or highlight _____

Step By Step

1.
2.
3.
4.
5.

Strategy-at-a-Glance

Strategy: *Stretch-a-Sentence*

Description: A strategy for highlighting key points in a story as a means to preview or review important ideas and words while using the sentence to build on learning.

Step-By-Step:

1. Begin by writing a sentence that will activate prior knowledge or provide an overview of the story to be read. The sentence should highlight key aspects of the text to reinforce a content area topic (*Caterpillars change into butterflies.; Spiders spin webs.*) or main idea of the story (*The hungry giant wants honey.; The tigers are loose.*). The initial sentence should be brief and simple, generally limited to five to seven words. New learning will be added to the sentence after reading by using the text as a springboard.

2. Write each word on an individual index card in large print with punctuation on a separate card. Additional blank cards will be used to add new words at the conclusion of the reading.

3. Introduce the story by giving a brief oral overview. Tell students that you have created a sentence to review these ideas (written in blue marker). Give each card to a child, taking a moment to identify the words on the cards before beginning. Ask students to arrange themselves in order to create a sentence that will reinforce the overview you provided. Read, reassemble and reread the sentence several times, creating a sort of "body cut-up sentence" as students make, break and recreate the sentence.

4. Display the sentence in clear view during reading. Draw attention back to the sentence as appropriate and remind students to think about additional details provided in the text. Key points may be listed on the board or this may be done after reading, depending largely on students and the complexity of the information.

5. After reading, students will reassemble the initial sentence. Discuss any new learning, encouraging students to think about words that could be added to reflect these ideas. Use a red marker to emphasize new learning, writing suggestions on individual cards so other students can stand in the appropriate place to *stretch* the sentence. *Caterpillars change into butterflies* may become *Caterpillars change into beautiful, colorful butterflies when they come out of the chrysalis. The tigers are loose* may become *The mean, hungry, ferocious tigers are loose in the zoo and people are frightened!* These changes provide many opportunities for rereading, vocabulary and punctuation (*"The wild tigers are loose!" yelled the zookeeper loudly.*). The initial sentence serves as a starting point while each *stretch* provides a new possibility for learning after reading.

6. Sentences may now be used as a buddy activity for repeated reading or new sentences may be added from related texts so that learning can be accumulated and organized. This provides time for review as well as to continuously initiate new learning.

Stretch a Sentence Form

Story/topic _____

The original sentence was

_____

_____

My Before Picture

The new sentence is

_____

My After Picture

51 ©2004 by Dr. Mary Howard

Stretch-a-Story

1.
2.
3.
4.
5.
6.

Step by Step

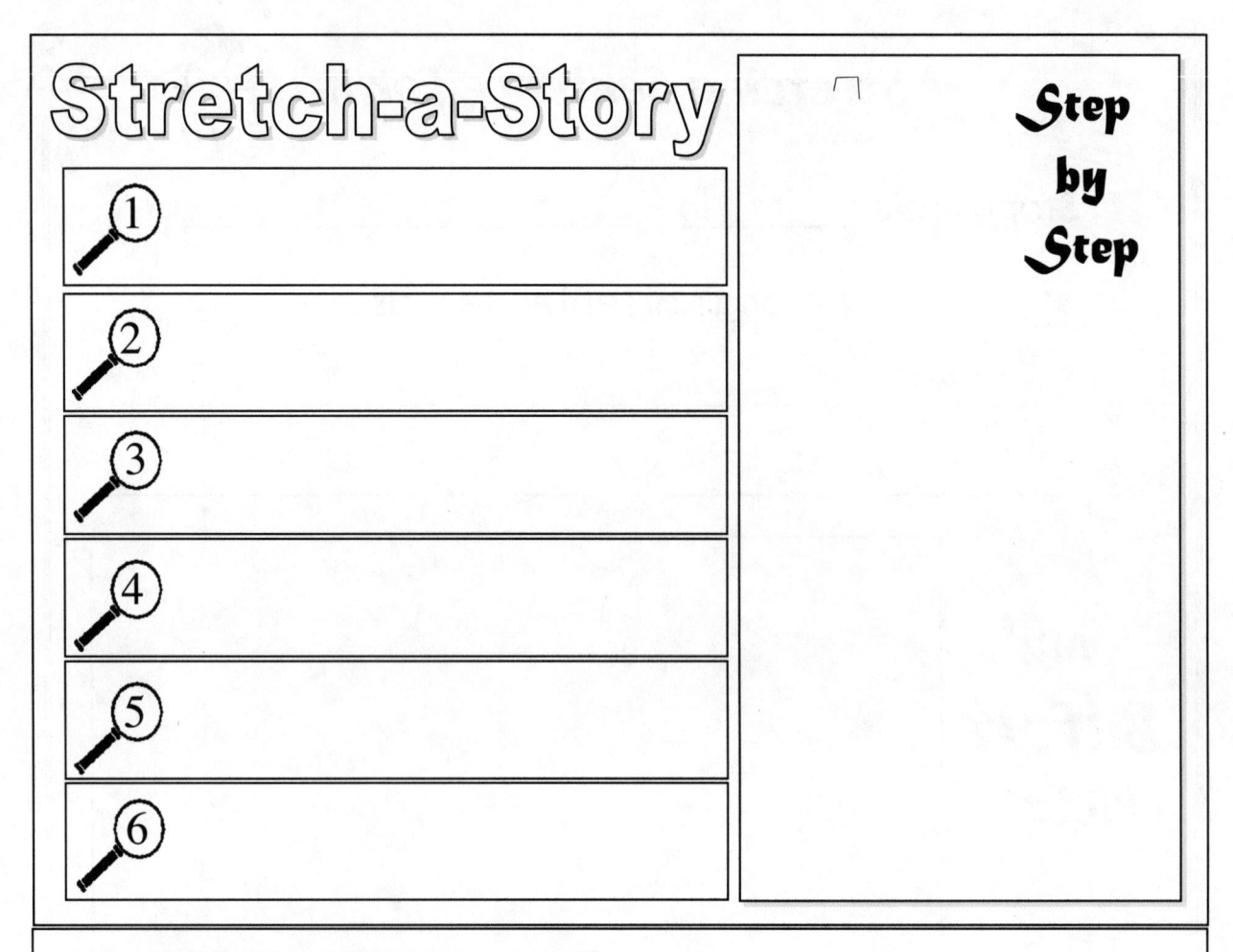

Extensions

- content area
- detail
- sequence
- step-by-step
- key ideas
- story map
- research
- timeline
- outline
- description

Strategy-at-a-Glance

Strategy: *Stretch-a-Story*

Description: A writing and revision strategy for breaking a written piece into more manageable chunks by creating a multi-page linear display that can be modified and *stretched* as new pages are added.

Step-By-Step:

1. Stretch-a-story always begins as a teacher-supported piece of writing, generally a language experience chart created in a small or whole group setting. This can follow any type of learning including a topic, story, or experience such as a class activity or field trip. Using a large piece of chart paper, the teacher acts as scribe by recording the children's language sequentially as it is verbalized. The initial writing serves as an outline while the end product provides a written record students can revisit for review and extension.

2. Because this has been done in a whole class setting and there are no visuals to support the print, it is likely to be more difficult for some children. This problem can be addressed after children leave that day by breaking the story into *manageable chunks*. In other words, the initial story is divided into individual portions with less print per page. Each portion is typically one or two sentences, although it may be a short paragraph for older students. Record sentences at the bottom of large pieces of construction paper, carefully printing words so that they can easily be read from a distance.

3. The following day, distribute pages for children to illustrate individually or through peer collaboration. Children are asked to carefully match the print to the picture. Notice that children are responsible for only a small section rather than the entire piece, so that each child will be able to participate successfully.

4. When the pages are finished, display them on the wall in a linear fashion for repeated rereading. This can be done as a buddy or independent reading first, providing time for children to practice the text and think about the sequence provided.

5. Children will now *stretch* the initial writing. After rereading, ask children if there are any details that have been left out. Once a specific event has been identified, record children's language on another piece of construction paper and ask for a volunteer to add a picture. Engage children in selecting where the additional page should go, literally moving pages so the new page can be added in sequence. This may be done daily for up to two weeks, rereading the pages on the wall to stretch it again and again as appropriate.

6. At the end of the writing, remove the pages from the wall and bind them together in book form. This will provide an ongoing resource for the experience that can be revisited independently or with a buddy. Notice that the language of children is preserved and reinforced in printed form while providing meaningful reading practice.

Stretch-a-Story
Reflection Form

My story is about

_____

_____

_____

I added these ideas to my story

- _____
- _____
- _____
- _____
- _____

I think I did a very good job stretching

_____

_____

_____

_____

©2004 by Dr. Mary Howard

Stretch-an-Idea

The Possibilities

beginning·middle·end

first·next·last

fact 1·fact 2·fact 3

point 1·point 2·point 3

who·wanted·but·so·finally

character·setting·problem·goal·resolution

Step By Step

1.
2.
3.
4.
5.

Strategy-at-a-Glance

Strategy: *Stretch-an-Idea*

Description: An outline strategy providing a means to visually organize thinking, using key words before writing to provide a skeletal view.

Step-By-Step:

1. Children will need a three by eighteen inch strip of white construction paper folded into five sections, with key words written at the top of each section. The key words will depend on the purpose. One is shown below, with alternatives such as *beginning, middle, end; first, second, third; fact one, fact two, fact three.*

Who	Wanted	But	So	Finally

2. The initial step depends on whether the activity is being used to retell a story or to provide an outline for personal writing. Children are asked to be brief, providing only key words and phrases for a skeletal view of the information. This condensed form will support the writing or retelling later, so should be simple and brief.

3. With the strip in clear view, students will complete each section. It is suggested that drawings are completed first, using the pictures as a guide to organize the print. This visual representation provides an overview as children add print details to each component. As appropriate, students may dictate ideas while the teacher records them on the form.

4. Once the skeleton is completed, children will now cut apart each section and lay them in sequential order. Pieces should be arranged in a linear fashion as shown so that children are able to see an overview of their initial thinking and what additions are needed. This makes it easy to revisit their first attempt as they plan what to add or modify. For beginning writers, the basic sections may be used as the story itself, although it is suggested that at least one detail is added as a model for early revision.

who	wanted	but	so	finally

5. Because each piece has been separated, it is easy for details to be added by moving pieces to insert an extension (stretch) as shown. Note that attention can be focused on one specific component at a time while key words provide an organizational guide. Pieces can now be put into book form just by stapling the pages together in sequence.

who		wanted	but	so		finally
	Stretch				*Stretch*	

Stretch-an-Idea
Reflection Form

These are the key ideas I can start with

- _____
- _____
- _____
- _____
- _____

Circle one of the ideas above to stretch

I can add these points

- _____
- _____
- _____
- _____
- _____

Something I learned is

_____
_____
_____

©2004 by Dr. Mary Howard

Reflective Pause #4

Do you cautiously select appropriate texts and tasks that consider children's needs and interests on a day-to-day basis?

Reinforced Current learning	Stimulated New learning

Critical Consideration #5

Focus on _____.

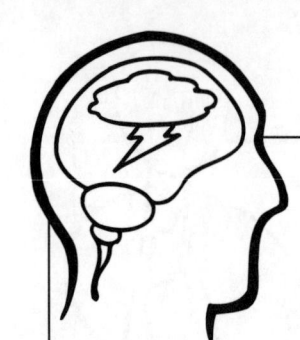

Two critical questions should guide every instructional decision:

- Will children be _____?

- Will children be _____ for that engagement?

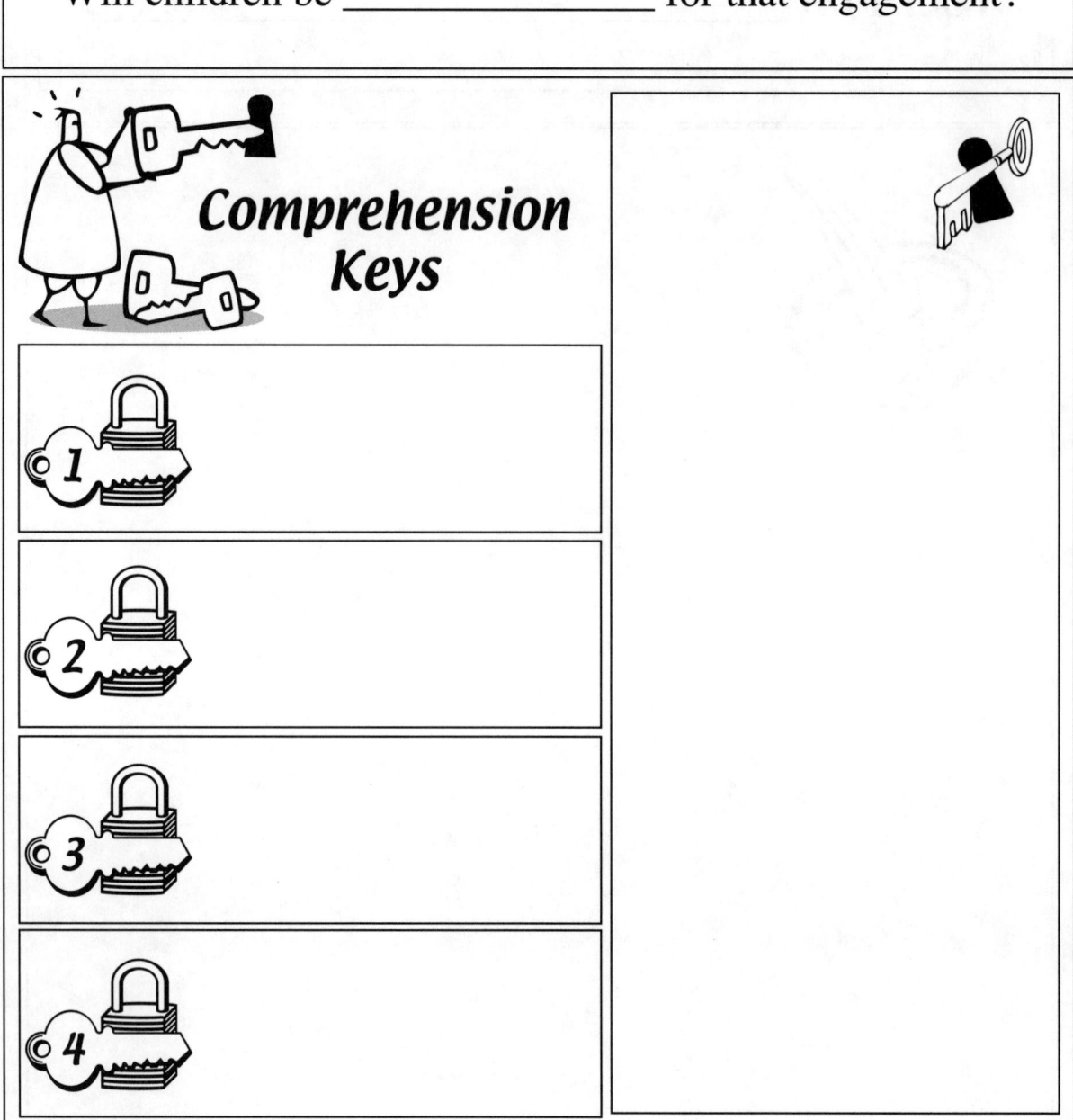

Comprehension Keys

1.

2.

3.

4.

Considerations for Effective Questioning

• Questions should be introduced before reading, displaying them in visible locations so they can be used to provide direction throughout reading. Discuss questions, drawing attention to key words and clues that will support thinking during and after reading. Encourage students to orally state the purpose for reading, supporting them as appropriate.

• Careful thought should always go into question selection, regardless of the source. Eliminate any that will not enhance understanding or provide an opportunity to teach a strategy. Avoid questions that focus attention on unimportant ideas as these tend to trivialize the reading process and reduce books to a mere regurgitation of facts and details.

• Exposure is an important aspect of learning. Unless children are exposed to high level questions, they will be unable to respond to them. Struggling readers are generally asked low level questions that focus on the details, with few experiences that model and reinforce higher level thinking. Emphasize questions that go beyond the book on a daily basis.

• Recall and comprehension are not the same thing, with memory a complicating factor for struggling readers. *Lookback,* or using the book to locate the answers, is always offered when responding to questions that pose memory demands. If a story is a teacher read-aloud, reread key selections first to support students in this process. The inability to merely call forth rote details is not a reflection on comprehension.

• Increase accountability by making students responsible for justifying and proving ideas and focusing on thinking, using the text as a valuable resource. Use probing to aid in verbalizing ideas (*Tell me more.; What do you mean?; Give me an example.*). Take advantage of teachable moments, offering both support and instruction whenever the opportunity arises.

• Questions should be designed to support and guide discussion rather than control it. Give children room to lead the discussion where it may take them, using questions only to refocus attention or give children *a good starting point.*

• It takes more comprehension to ask good questions than to answer them, making student-generated questions an important goal in the questioning process. Provide substantial modeling to demonstrate how both the text and outside sources such as prior knowledge and experience can be used in this process to build meaning.

• Teach children to think critically by responding to questions through teacher think-aloud (*When I read this question, it reminded me about how I felt when _____; I'm not sure exactly what the question is asking, but I wonder if _____*) and to analyze questions (*Is the question worth asking?; How could it be reworded to make it a better question?; Restate the question in your own words.; Is there a better question to ask?*). This support will form a bridge to increasing independence while providing rich instructional opportunities.

Questioning Prompts

Focus on Meaning
Semantic Knowledge

- Did that make sense?
- What is happening in the story?
- What happened in the story when _____?
- What do you think may happen next?
- What would you expect _____ to say next?
- What do you think that word could be?
- Look at the picture. What is happening?
- What would make sense there?
- Cover the word and predict what it could be.
- Try _____. Would that make sense?

Focus on Structure
Syntactic Knowledge

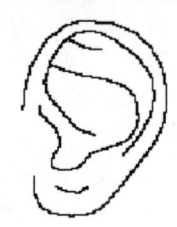

- Did that sound right?
- Does that sound the way we talk?
- You said _____. Can we say it that way?
- Would it be correct to say _____?
- Is there a better way to say it?
- Can you think of a better word?
- What word would sound right there?
- What is another word that might fit?
- Could you say it another way?
- Try _____. Would that sound right?

Focus on Visual
Graphophonic Knowledge

- Did that look right?
- Do you know a word that starts/ends with those letters?
- Reread it and get your mouth ready for that word.
- What do you notice about that word?
- Could that word be _____?
- Does it look like _____?
- Do you see a part of the word you know?
- Do you know a word that could help you?
- Do you think it looks like _____?
- Try _____. Would that look like the word?

My Strategy Bookmark

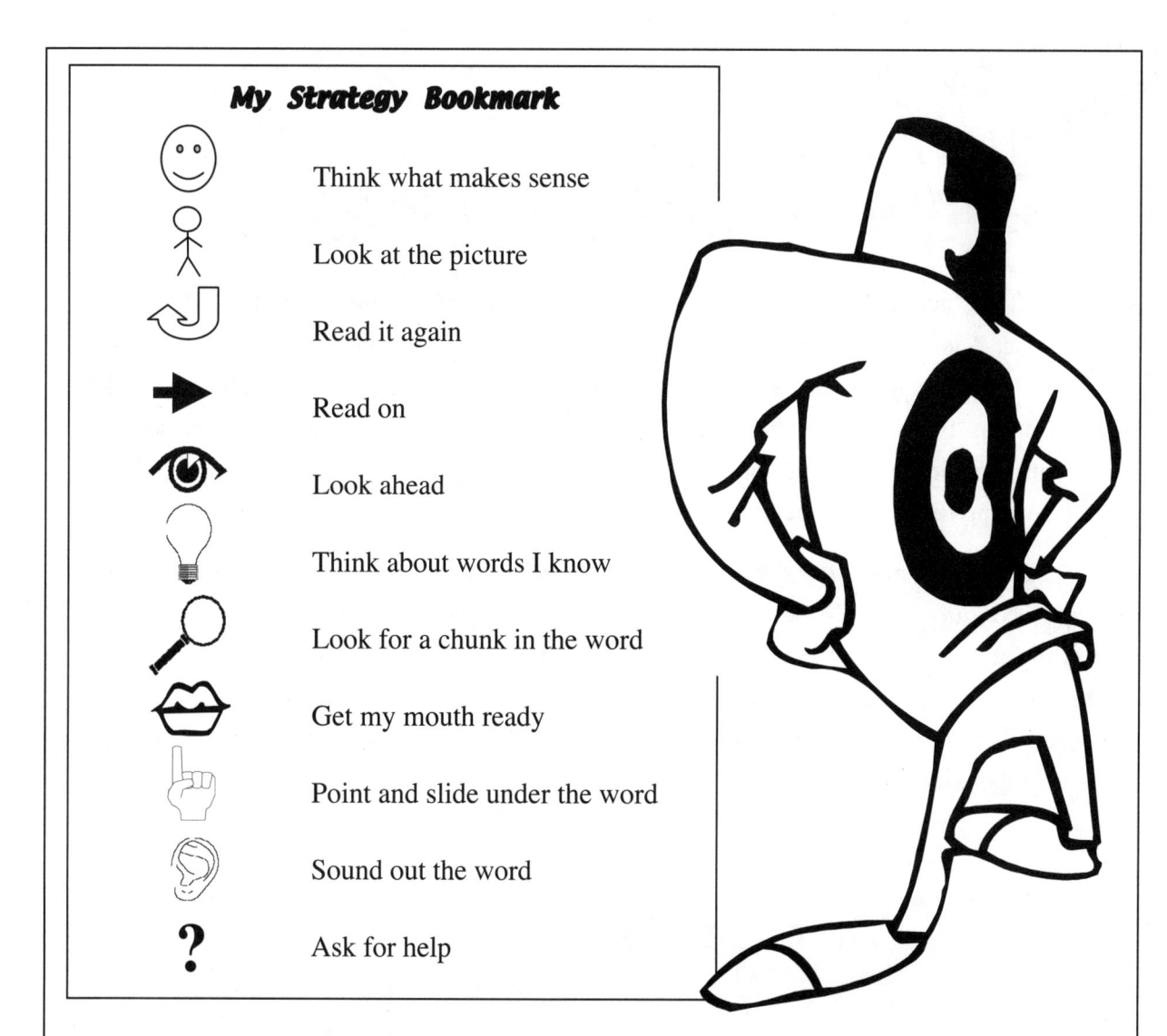

- 😊 Think what makes sense
- 🚶 Look at the picture
- ↩ Read it again
- ➡ Read on
- 👁 Look ahead
- 💡 Think about words I know
- 🔍 Look for a chunk in the word
- 👄 Get my mouth ready
- ☝ Point and slide under the word
- 👂 Sound out the word
- ❓ Ask for help

A *Strategy Bookmark* allows specific strategies to be highlighted and reinforced as children are in the process of learning them. The bookmark makes strategies easily accessible, allowing the teacher to draw attention to examples in a variety of contexts. Engage students in adding new strategies to the bookmark during the year, frequently revisiting the bookmark to reinforce strategies during reading. The bookmark format offers many benefits such as:

- easy for the brain to process
- offers a visual representation of strategies
- reinforces current knowledge
- prompts for specific strategies
- encourages independent application
- enhances recall
- promotes think-aloud
- allows gradual withdrawal

A Changing Focus

When students cannot respond to a question, reading comprehension is not always the issue. There may be a variety of contributing factors, ranging from a poorly stated question, a language processing problem or poor recall. These problems can be addressed by restating the question (alternate language), selecting a new question (perhaps more appropriate), integrating a student initiated retelling (an overview of main story points) or providing lookback (using the book to locate answers).

Student-generated questions should be the ultimate goal over teacher or publisher generated questions. These personal questions will help children think through the reading and provide valuable assessment information not available through questions that come from outside sources. This makes one question worthy of inclusion and gives students a chance to show what they know rather than what outside sources want them to regurgitate!

What question

do you _____

I had asked you

so you could show me

_____

about this story or topic?

My Self-Questioning Form

The question I wish you had asked me is

_____
_____
_____

I think this is a good question because

_____
_____
_____

I would answer this question by

_____
_____
_____

I think this question demonstrates understanding by

_____
_____

©2004 by Dr. Mary Howard

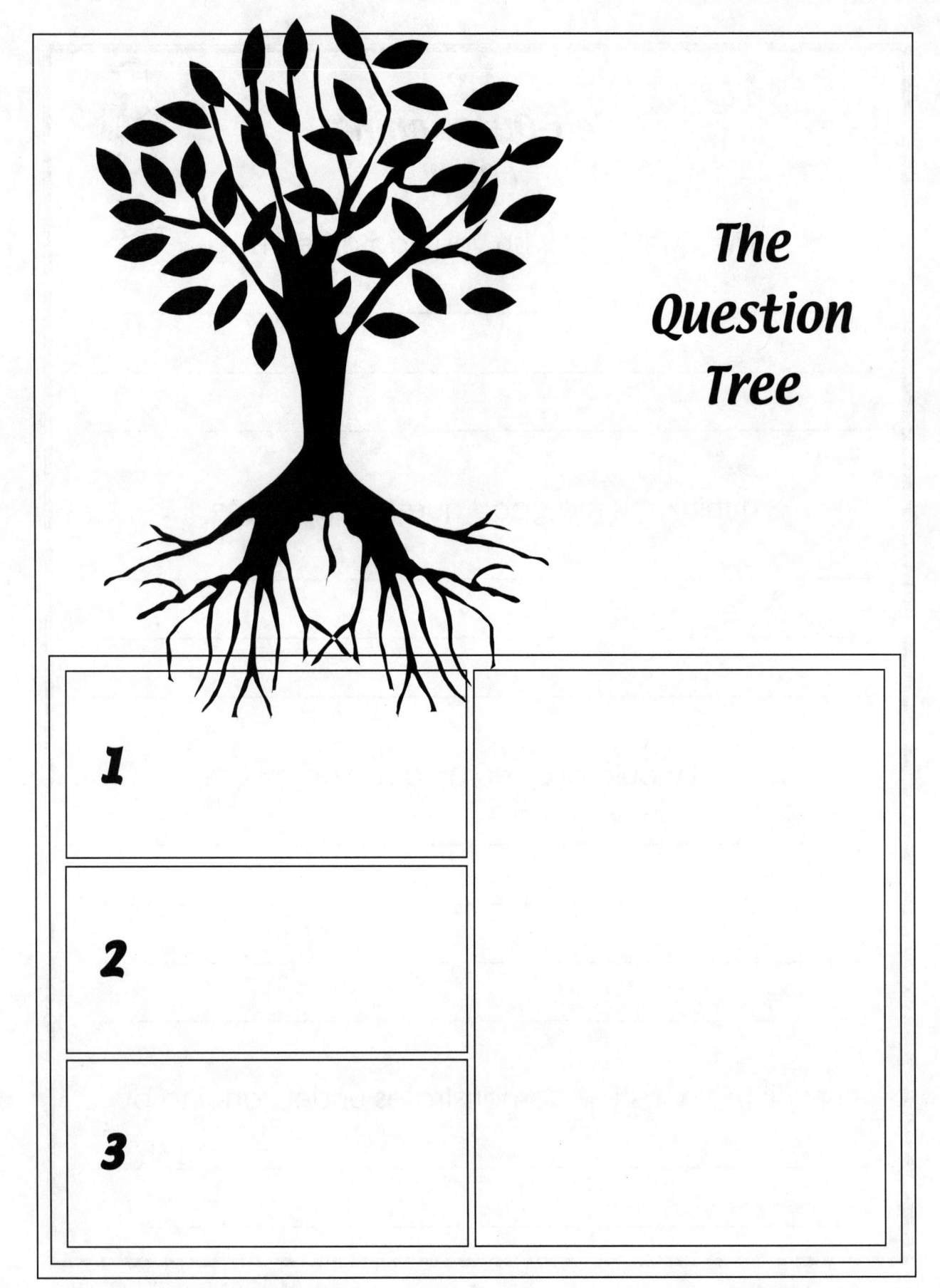

The Question Tree

1

2

3

Questioning Categories

Above the Surface (branches)

The answers to *Above the Surface* questions can be found in the text so that the reader can highlight, underline or read aloud directly from the print. They are explicit or literal questions for locating specific information. Questions often begin with *who, what, when* or *where*.

On the Surface (grass)

The answers to *On the Surface* questions are also located in the text, but they may not be stated directly or in one place. Answers may be embedded, inferred or between the lines, but rarely in a single location. Questions may also begin with *who, what, when* or *where*, just as those found in *Below the Surface* questions.

Below the Surface (roots)

The answers to *Below the Surface* questions come from a variety of sources including the text, the reader and the author. Some questions can be answered without the text, but always require the reader to go beyond the print while using it to support and guide thinking. Questions often begin with *how, why, could, should,* or *would*.

Strategy-at-a-Glance

Strategy: *Question Tree*

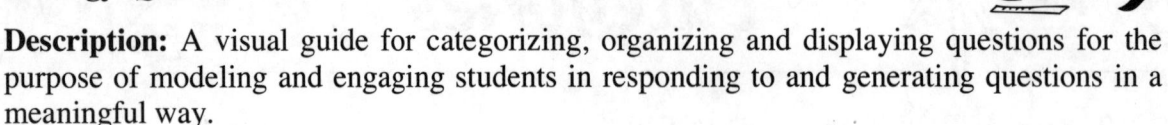

Description: A visual guide for categorizing, organizing and displaying questions for the purpose of modeling and engaging students in responding to and generating questions in a meaningful way.

Step-By-Step:

1. Begin by creating the question tree on an enlarged chart that will remain on the wall all year. The three question variations will be labeled on the tree using the descriptions shown (*Above the Surface* [branches]; *On the Surface* [grass]; *Below the Surface* [roots]). Take time to discuss the purpose and characteristics of each questioning category.

2. Ample teacher modeling will provide a clear understanding of the process before children generate questions of their own. Begin by selecting only a few questions following a story, with at least one or two represented at each level. Write each question on individual index cards, reading it aloud and verbalizing where it belongs on the tree and why (*The first question is What is the name of the inventor who made the discovery? I'm going to put this question Above the Surface because I know I can find the answer directly in the book. I will have to use the book to find this answer*).

3. Once children understand the various categories, demonstrate how to respond to questions meaningfully. Read the question orally, thinking aloud as you respond (*What is the question asking me? Where will I find the answer to this question?*) while using the book as appropriate. Demonstrate how questions may be reworded to clarify what is being asked (*I think the question is asking me _____*).

4. Teacher modeling can vary from one or two weeks to one or two months, depending on the prior knowledge and experiences children bring with them. Gradually engage students in the process of generating questions of their own. Varying degrees of support can be offered in whole or small groups or on a one-to-one basis. Also guide children in categorizing questions on the tree and in formulating meaningful responses.

5. The next step is for children to begin responding to personal questions by continuing this shared process. Read each question aloud, asking children what the question is asking. This begins as a whole group, but provide opportunities to work with a partner as soon as possible. Record responses as children answer questions and place them on the tree in the appropriate location, encouraging them to verbalize these choices.

6. The final goal is independence, gradually relinquishing responsibility to children after ample modeled (teacher demonstration), shared (with the teacher) and guided (student control with teacher support) experiences. Students will eventually assume full control of generating and responding to questions independently. Questions may also be placed on color-coded cards on the tree [*must do* (red) and *can do* (green)] as appropriate.

Question Tree
Self-Questioning Form

Title/Topic _____

Above the Surface Question

• _____

On the Surface Question

• _____

Below the Surface Question

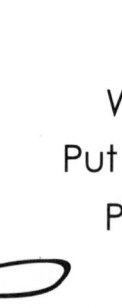

• _____

Write your questions on an index card.
Put your answer on the back of each card.
Put the questions on the question tree.

©2004 by Dr. Mary Howard

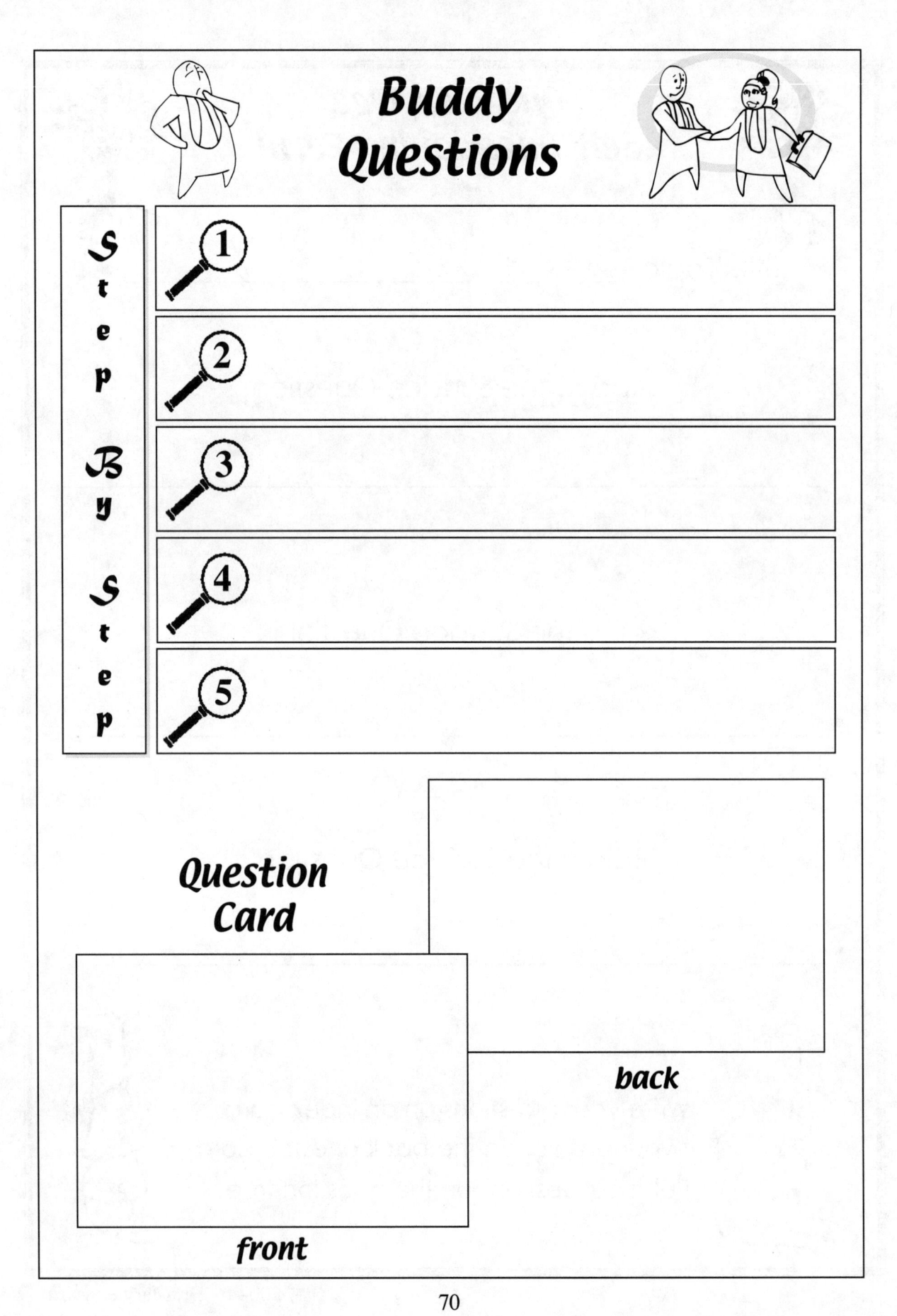

Buddy Questions

Step By Step

1.
2.
3.
4.
5.

Question Card

front

back

Strategy-at-a-Glance

Strategy: *Buddy Questions*

Description: A questioning strategy pairing two children who have read the same book in order to formulate, exchange and respond to self-selected questions collaboratively, by assuming the role of both coach and cheerleader.

Step-By-Step:

1. Buddy questions provide a collaborative way to revisit a self-selected text through student-generated questions. The text may be easy or one that offers a few challenges, but it is *never* a frustration text for either child. Understanding must be high for the procedure to be effective. Texts should be at an appropriate level and one that both students are motivated to revisit so that engagement is high. Each child completes the initial reading before the procedure begins, although reading may occur independently or with the buddy. Encourage a second reading if needed for increased understanding.

2. Once both children have read the text and have had a few minutes to revisit key ideas, they work independently to create one or two questions that will help connect to important events and ideas. Students will design questions to meaningfully reengage the responder in the text by drawing attention to key concepts rather than irrelevant points. These questions may be randomly selected by students or related to a specific focus such as the characters or story problem. Encourage questions that promote a deeper understanding of the reading, avoiding yes/no questions or those requiring simple one word answers. Effective questions encourage the reader to rethink the reading by combining the text and personal knowledge. Questions are recorded on the index card, with one question on each card.

3. Buddy supports are recorded on the other side of the index card. These supports may include page numbers, key words and phrases. Key points in the book may be marked with sticky notes to aid the discussion, draw attention to specific text, provide examples, or highlight the essential concepts. An optional form has been provided for this purpose.

4. When students have generated the questions and marked the text, questions are exchanged. Children now take turns responding to the buddy question, using the book in this process. It is the responsibility of each buddy to support the response in any way necessary, returning to marked sections in the book or reading a selection aloud *(Remember the part in the story where she first decided to stay? Read this paragraph again. It will help you answer my question.).*

5. When questions are answered, buddies are asked to record key points on the form provided. Additional questions that may have been helpful may also be listed *(What other questions would you expect someone to be able to answer if they have understood the book?).* The primary benefit comes from reflecting on the role questions play in building meaning, so responding to them is optional and considered secondary.

Buddy Question Planning Form

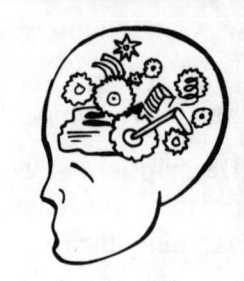

My buddy question is

_____
_____
_____

These pages will help my buddy answer the question

_____ _____ _____ _____

I can use these key words and ideas to help my buddy

_____   _____

_____   _____

_____   _____

I think a good answer to my question is

_____
_____
_____
_____
_____

©2004 by Dr. Mary Howard

Buddy Questions

Buddy #1 _____

Buddy #2 _____

Title _____

Buddy Question #1	Buddy Question #2
Answer #1	Answer #2

More Questions worth asking

©2004 by Dr. Mary Howard

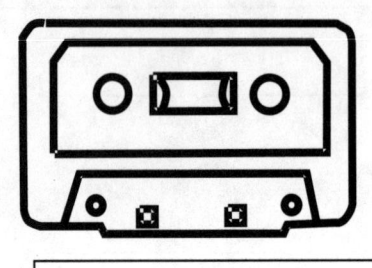

Quick Tapes

General Description

Contents

1.

2.

Optional extension

Assessment Source

Strategy-at-a-Glance

Strategy: *Quick Tapes*

Description: A quick strategy to initiate a brief oral summary and self-selected repeated reading, using high motivation texts for reinforcement and assessment purposes.

Step-By-Step:

1. There is a direct correlation between increased motivation and engagement. For this reason, Quick Tapes are always self-selected texts. These selections are based on interest, using any source, for the purpose of building meaning and fluency. This also provides an excellent assessment tool for identifying the appropriateness of independent reading selections, for strategies learned and in progress, and for fluency and comprehension.

2. Each child will need a ten minute tape. With five minutes of recording length on each side, these are perfect for completing a brief but meaningful reading. Ten minute tapes can be purchased inexpensively from Crystal Springs Publishing Co. (www.crystalsprings.com). It is preferable that each child has a personal tape which can be stored in a reading folder and reused. Four to six children can rotate through the taping center each day so a tape is completed for each child during the week.

3. Any text can become a Quick Tape as long as it is at an appropriate level so meaning is high. The selection should be read prior to completing the tape. One benefit of the Quick Tape is the limited time involved (five minutes), minimizing the negative role of attention. There are essentially two parts for each tape: the introduction or summary and the reading itself. The child always introduces the book by giving the title, author and a brief summary. The summary can be an overview of the story, including, for a longer book, a lead-in for the reading (*I read a story about_____; I'm going to read the part of the story where_____*). For an expository reading, this may be a summary of one or several facts about the topic. After the overview, the child reads for the remainder of the tape, generally a little over four minutes. This provides ample time to practice without allowing boredom to set in. It will also provide an adequate sample for teacher assessment purposes.

4. Side 2 is optional, providing a good source for reflection and self assessment. This side can be used for a more fluent second rendition if the child desires, providing repetition and reinforcement since the same selection is read a second time. If time allows, the student may choose to do this after listening to the first reading, completing the second reading for the purpose of improving it.

5. It is recommended that one tape per child is targeted for teacher assessment each month. This will provide a quick survey of the child's ability to select appropriate texts, condense the text into a brief overview and read the story with a high level of accuracy and fluency. As appropriate, the teacher may meet with individual children to reinforce specific features of the reading, to select a teaching point such as a miscue or the sample choice, or to show evidence of fluency or the suitability of the selection for independent practice.

Quick Tape

My story is about

_____
_____
_____

The part of the story I decided to record is about

_____
_____
_____

I chose to read this part of the story because

_____
_____
_____

I think I did a very good job in the following ways

_____
_____
_____

©2004 by Dr. Mary Howard

Reflective Pause #5

Do you place a focus on teaching critical strategies for thinking that emphasize process over product?

Reinforced Current learning	Stimulated New learning

Taking a TRIP Down Memory Lane

T

R

I

P

Big Picture

Part 1:

Maxims for Word Learning

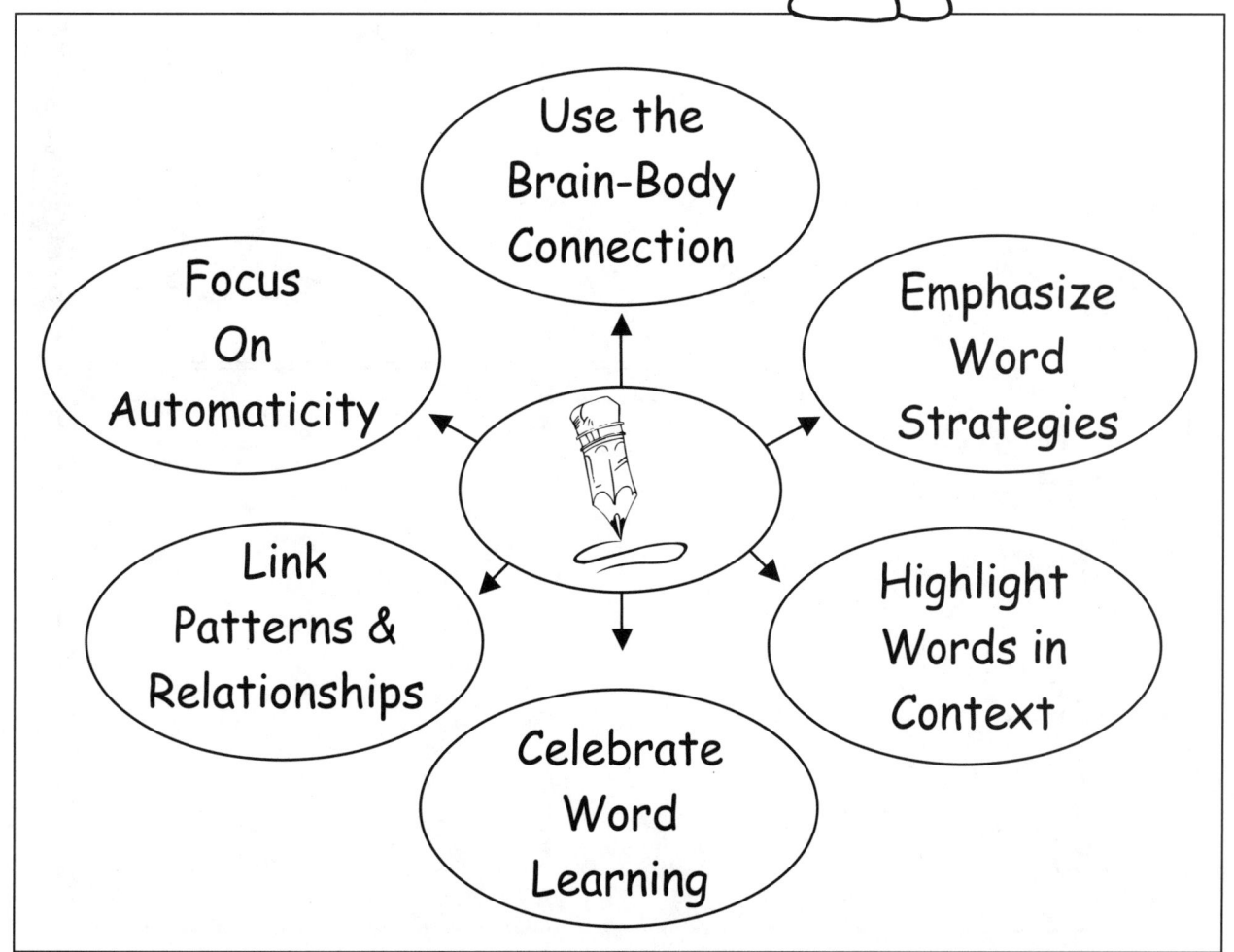

- Use the Brain-Body Connection
- Focus On Automaticity
- Emphasize Word Strategies
- Link Patterns & Relationships
- Highlight Words in Context
- Celebrate Word Learning

Making Words Memor**able**

High Priority Words

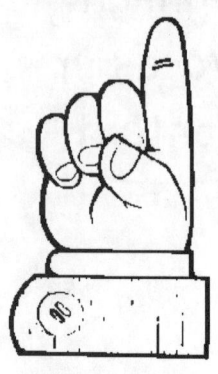

Make the _____ Connection

Maxim #1

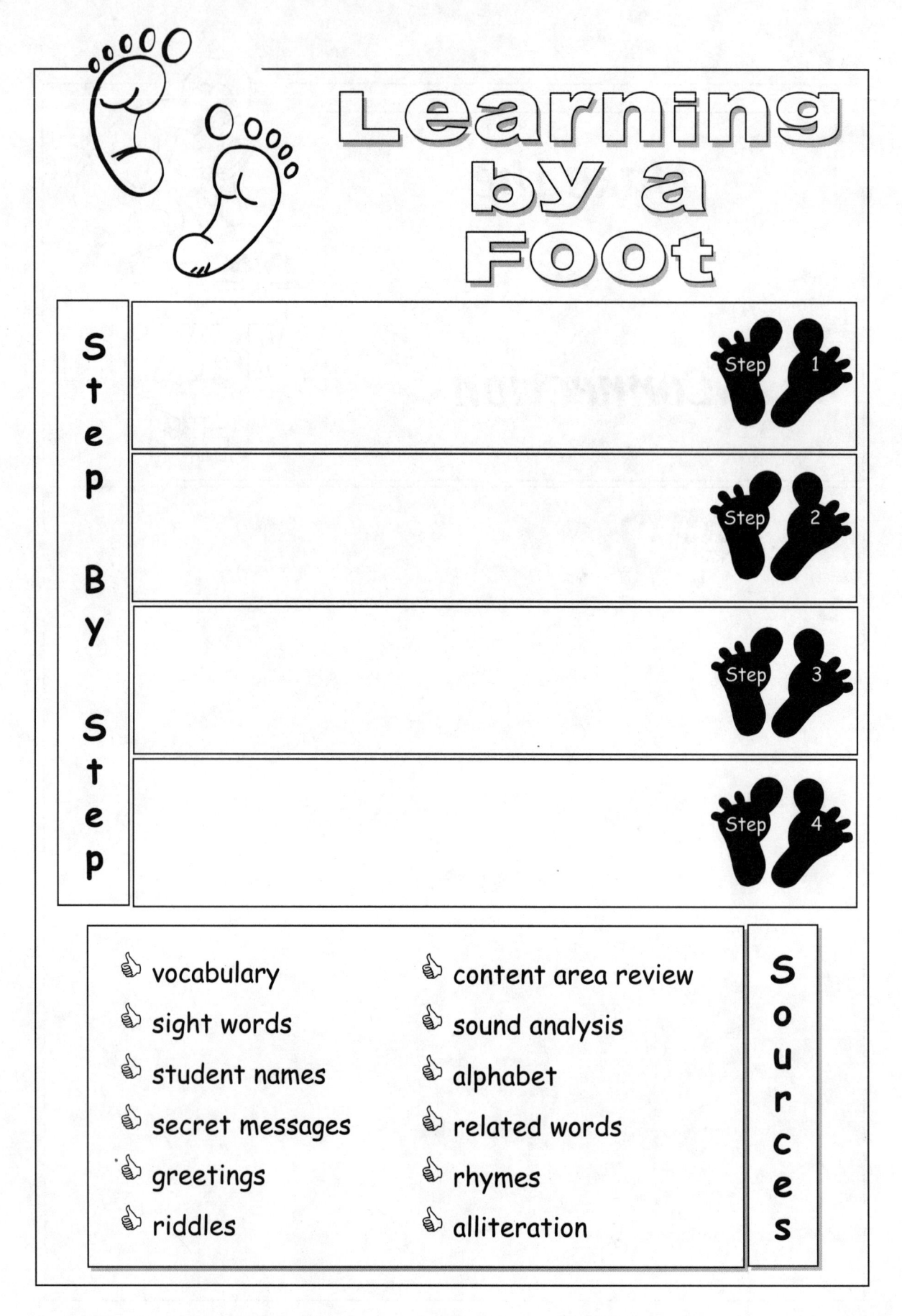

Learning by a Foot

Step By Step

Step 1

Step 2

Step 3

Step 4

Sources

- 👍 vocabulary
- 👍 sight words
- 👍 student names
- 👍 secret messages
- 👍 greetings
- 👍 riddles
- 👍 content area review
- 👍 sound analysis
- 👍 alphabet
- 👍 related words
- 👍 rhymes
- 👍 alliteration

Strategy-at-a-Glance

Strategy: *Learning by a Foot*

Description: A strategy for promoting opportunities to practice high frequency words through movement and repetition in a meaningful context.

Step-By-Step:

1. Learning by a Foot is a pleasurable way to practice words in the context of a meaningful sentence while adding movement for greater recall. The goal is to reinforce and build sight vocabulary using a complete sentence or idea as the source. Sentences may be repetitive to reinforce a specific word (*I like to play games; I like to jump up and down; I like to run fast.*); review a concept *(Spiders have eight legs.; Black widows are poisonous.);* summarize a story children have read or listened to *(Goldilocks went to the house of the three bears.; The giant wants honey and butter.);* or simply convey a message *(Have a great day!; I am so glad you're here!; Meet me in the reading center.).* Create sentences that will reinforce what children know as you build a bridge to new word learning in the process.

2. Designate a specific area in the room away from the main traffic as the walking center. This may be a path along the side of the room, by the library center or next to the doorway. Students will be walking on footprints, so word cards should be laminated and covered with a plastic sheet such as a strip of laminating film. The sheet can be taped on three sides so footprints can easily be slipped in and out for a new sentence.

3. Print each word in the sentence on a footprint cut from poster board or sturdy cardstock, using large and legible letters. A picture may be added to the heel as appropriate to support new or challenging words. If the sentence will reinforce a concept, key words or chunks may be coded in red (*Spiders have **eight** legs.; The **fat** cat **sat** on a **mat**.*). Footprints can now be stored and reused.

4. Arrange footprints in the proper order to make the desired sentence, making sure footprints move from right to left and bottom to top as shown.

5. Footprints are now ready for student practice. A time can be designated during the day for students to "walk and read" independently or with a buddy, although the beauty of the procedure is the simplicity and ease. A child can walk and read on the way to sharpen a pencil or select a book, practicing words as they go. While it may take a few seconds more to reach the final destination, the repeated reading is time well spent as children practice words and have fun in the process!

6. Sentences are generally used for one week to allow for needed repetition of words. Students may also generate sentences to summarize a story or topic, adding to the benefit of the process.

Drastic Strategy

Getting Started

from	Select one _____ word
from (in hand)	_____ the word in context
from (magnetic)	_____ magnetic letters
(pencil)	Write the word from _____
(clock)	Revisit the word _____

Strategy-at-a-Glance

Strategy: *Drastic Strategy* (adapted from Cunningham, 1980)

Description: A strategy for enhancing recall of high frequency words through repetition and multi-modal sensory input.

Step-By-Step:

1. Identify the target word, or a high frequency word children are having difficulty learning. Drastic Strategy is intended for a small group format of one to five children who would benefit from multi-modal repetition. Each member of the group will need a personal word card (3 x 5 index card), with the target word printed on both sides. Each child will also need the magnetic letters used to form the target word.

2. Use the target word repeatedly in a meaningful story as children look at the word card. Talk at a slow but expressive pace, emphasizing the word each time you come to it (*There once was a young princess from another land. One day she moved from her kingdom…*). Each time children hear the word, the card is raised overhead with eyes following the word. Notice that several modalities are addressed, including visual (*Look at the word*), auditory (*Listen for the word*) and tactile-kinesthetic (*Hold up the word when you hear it*).

3. Reverse the role by letting children take turns creating a story or sentences as other members of the group hold up the word card. Since the word is written on both sides of the card, every student is able to see the word as it is raised. Verbalizing the word in sentences adds an additional component to the process.

4. Each child manipulates the magnetic letters to *make-and-break* the word several times by reassembling the letters in the correct order. This should be done without hesitation, reminding the child to slide a finger under each letter when the word is formed while slowly verbalizing it. The word is then reassembled and reread five or six times.

5. Children will write the word from memory without a print model in view. Remind them to begin by looking at the word card carefully to get it in their mind, sliding a finger under it while saying the word slowly. The word is then covered so it can be printed correctly from memory. If the child hesitates or tries to sound the word out, uncover and try again. The child should be able to write the word accurately and without hesitation from memory, erasing and rewriting the word several times in this way. Use the model as needed, repeating the word until it can be written five or six times without the model.

6. Provide time to revisit the target word by locating it in books or other print sources. *Reading the room* is an excellent strategy, giving children a pointer so that they can locate, point, and read the target word with a partner. A variety of print sources to reinforce word knowledge should be displayed around the room for this purpose. Provide many opportunities to meet the word in meaningful texts over time. Reinforcement is the key!

Reflective Pause #1

Do you provide strategies that activate multiple pathways for learning new words by engaging the body in this process?

Reinforced Current learning	Stimulated New learning

Promote

Increasing

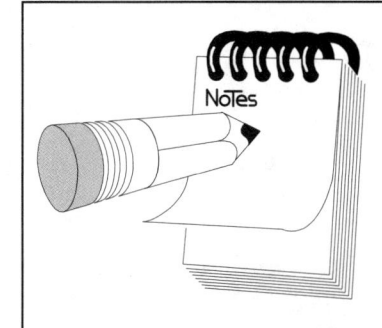

_____

Maxim #2

The Maze

Designate _____ areas, varying the _____ and _____, and using different writing _____ and _____.

The Words

Select _____ _____ word to build a reading & writing _____.

The Strategy

Fluency Practice Maze

Strategy-at-a-Glance

Strategy: *Fluency Practice Maze*

Description: A quick strategy for placing high priority words into long-term memory through rote practice, repetition and drill.

Step-By-Step:

1. Begin by creating a practice maze, designating four to six writing surfaces in the room that are at different heights and planes where children will practice the target word. Begin the drill with a dry erase board, positioning it slightly above eye level. Other writing areas may include a chart stand, desk, blackboard or small dry erase boards stationed in varying locations and angles in the room. Each station contains a blank writing surface with a variety of writing utensils in varied colors ready to use. Writing areas should be in closer proximity to one another for younger students, while they may be located on opposite sides of the room, perhaps in each of the four corners, for older students. The child's desk is the final stopping point, where a writing surface awaits.

2. This strategy is designed to maximize word learning in a game format through rapid repetition and drill. Only one word will be targeted at a time so the focus is on *that* word. It is important that *priority* words, specifically high frequency or high utility words, take precedence. Explain to children that they will be asked to write the word on each of the surfaces located in the maze, *holding the word in their head* while moving from place to place to write the word again. The teacher is stationed at the first point only to initiate the writing and make sure that the word is written correctly.

3. As soon as the child writes the word, erase it and repeat this at least five or six times on different locations on the board. If the child stops to think about or sound out the word or if it is written incorrectly, erase the word and write it slowly as the child watches to provide a model. Ask the child to run one finger under the word, reading it while looking at each letter as it is verbalized. Erase the word and ask the child to begin again. The idea is to write the word accurately, repeatedly, and without hesitation.

4. When the word has been written several times correctly, the child dashes to the next location to write the word on the awaiting surface. The word is written only once this time before the student moves on again. The teacher is checking strictly for accuracy rather than following the child around the room to erase words. The end of the maze is the child's desk, where the word is promptly written for a final time.

5. When the maze is completed, return to each writing area to check and celebrate the word. Fluency Practice Maze is brief, generally taking about one to three minutes to complete. This makes it easy to repeat throughout the week. Once students are familiar with the procedure, it can be used as an independent or buddy activity, providing continued practice and reinforcement.

Spelling Practice Folder

	1	2	3	4	5

Look

Cover

Write

Check

Repeat

Strategy-at-a-Glance

Strategy: *Spelling Fluency Folder*

Description: A ready-to-use procedure for home, independent or buddy spelling practice with a focus on building automaticity for long-term word learning.

Step-By-Step:

1. The goal of word learning should always be to place words in long-term memory. This does not occur through low-level, time-wasting activities that focus on rote recall, such as copying words, but through strategies that aid in coding words into visual memory. Spelling Fluency Folder is an easy way to promote permanent word learning. Each child will need a personal spelling folder that can be created easily and inexpensively using manila file folders. (Because this is an excellent activity for home practice as well, it is recommended that two folders are created for each child so one can be used at home.) The folder can take two forms, depending on grade level. The horizontal version is generally used beyond the early grades because the small space provided for each word is adequate. For younger writers, the folder can be turned vertically so that a larger space is provided for writing words. In each case, six flaps will be cut and labeled as shown.

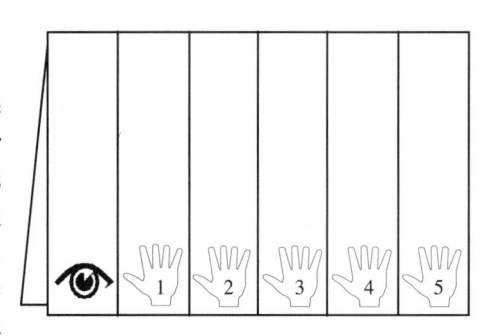

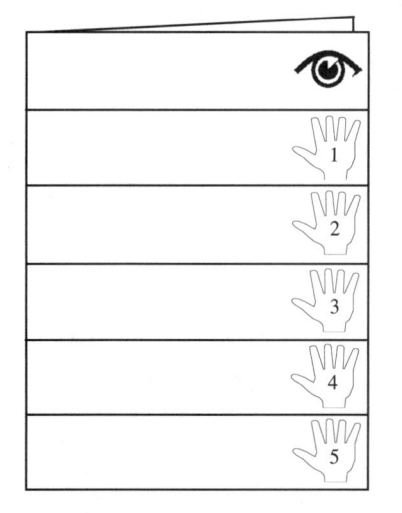

2. A strip of paper will be needed for each word, selecting only five to seven words for this activity. These provide the visual model for the words and a place for students to write. To make the horizontal folder, cut sheets of unlined white paper in fourths horizontally. For the vertical folder, full sheets of paper will be used. Write one word on the left side of the horizontal sheets and at the top of the vertical pages. Words are always written clearly in their printed form as they are easier to commit to visual memory in print rather than cursive. Strips are then placed inside the folder so the word will be seen when the child opens the first flap (eye). Be sure that the words will fit in the space provided. This model will be used prior to writing the word each time.

Spelling Fluency Folder: Continued

3. The child begins by lifting the first flap (eye), looking closely at the word to code it into visual memory. Let children maintain control, as some children will need to see the word only briefly while others will need to focus attention on the word longer. The model is *not to* be in view during writing because this is not a copying activity, so the flap is closed before moving to the next step. The first numbered flap (1) is then lifted so the word can be written from memory. This sequence is repeated, always returning to the original model before writing, until the word has been written five times to provide repeated exposure to each word. If a word is misspelled, the child simply draws a line through it and continues to the next flap. When all five steps have been completed, the strip is removed from the folder and a new one is created for the same word. The child will then repeat the word until it can be written correctly all five times. This will provide important repetition without making it a copying activity.

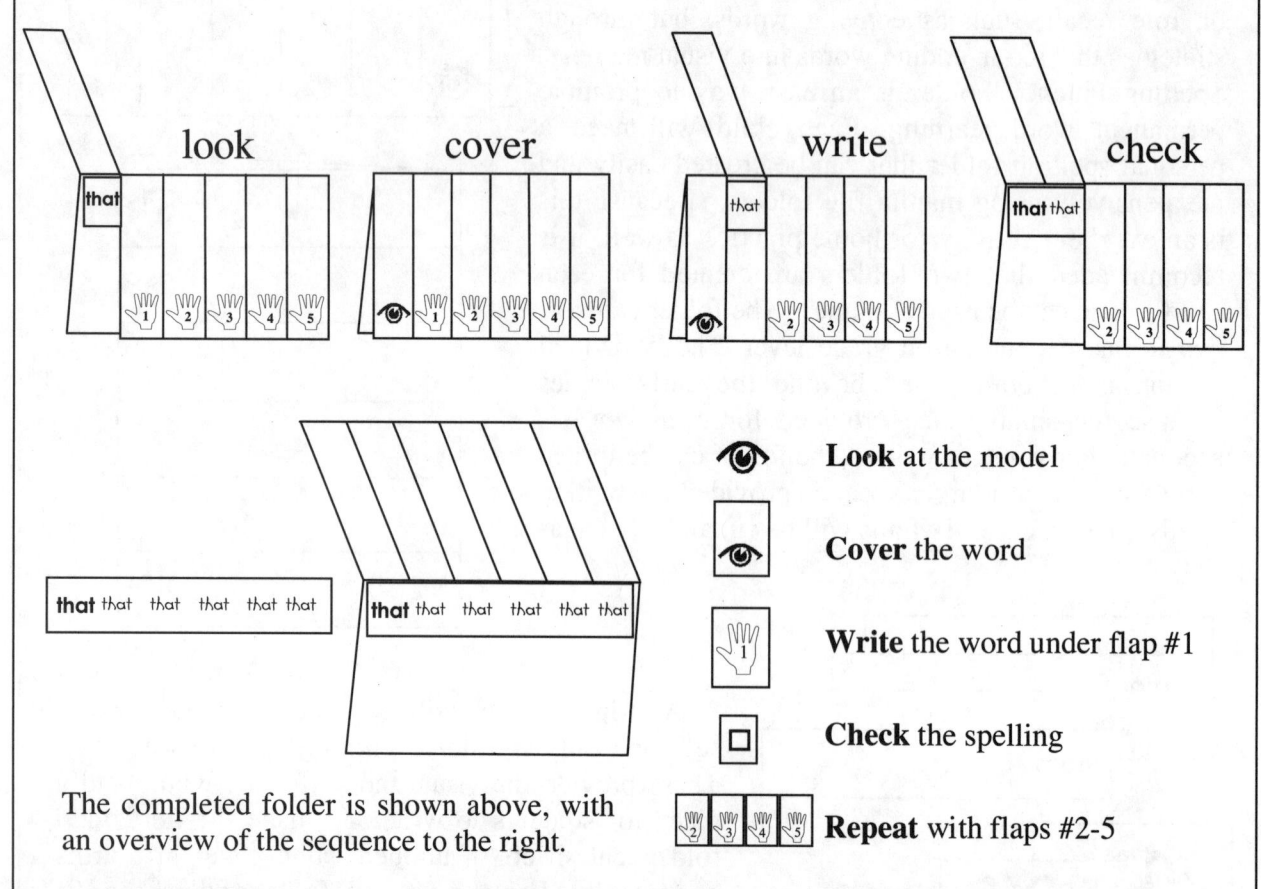

look   cover   write   check

The completed folder is shown above, with an overview of the sequence to the right.

- **Look** at the model
- **Cover** the word
- **Write** the word under flap #1
- **Check** the spelling
- **Repeat** with flaps #2-5

4. Because the focus is on coding words into memory, children can maximize the benefits simply by pausing for several seconds before writing each word. This will force them to hold the word in visual memory a little longer. Encourage children to be creative by adding their own twists like walking around the table before writing it again or counting to ten. Anything that allows them to hold onto the word a bit longer will be effective.

5. Another component can be added to this procedure by using magnetic letters to make-and-break the word. The child will use the letters to make each word, forming and reforming them several times without hesitation.

My Word Learning Contract

I want to read and write this word from memory

I am going to do these things to learn my word

- _____
- _____
- _____
- _____
- _____

I will show that I know my word in this way

_____
_____

❏ I am learning my word　　❏ I learned my word

©2004 by Dr. Mary Howard

Reflective Pause #2

Do you emphasize building a growing store of reading and writing sight vocabulary over skill-and-drill practices?

Reinforced Current learning

Stimulated New learning

Focus on _____

For word learning

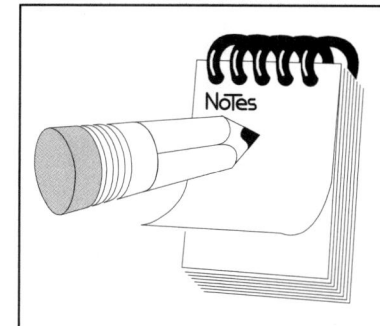

Maxim #3

front

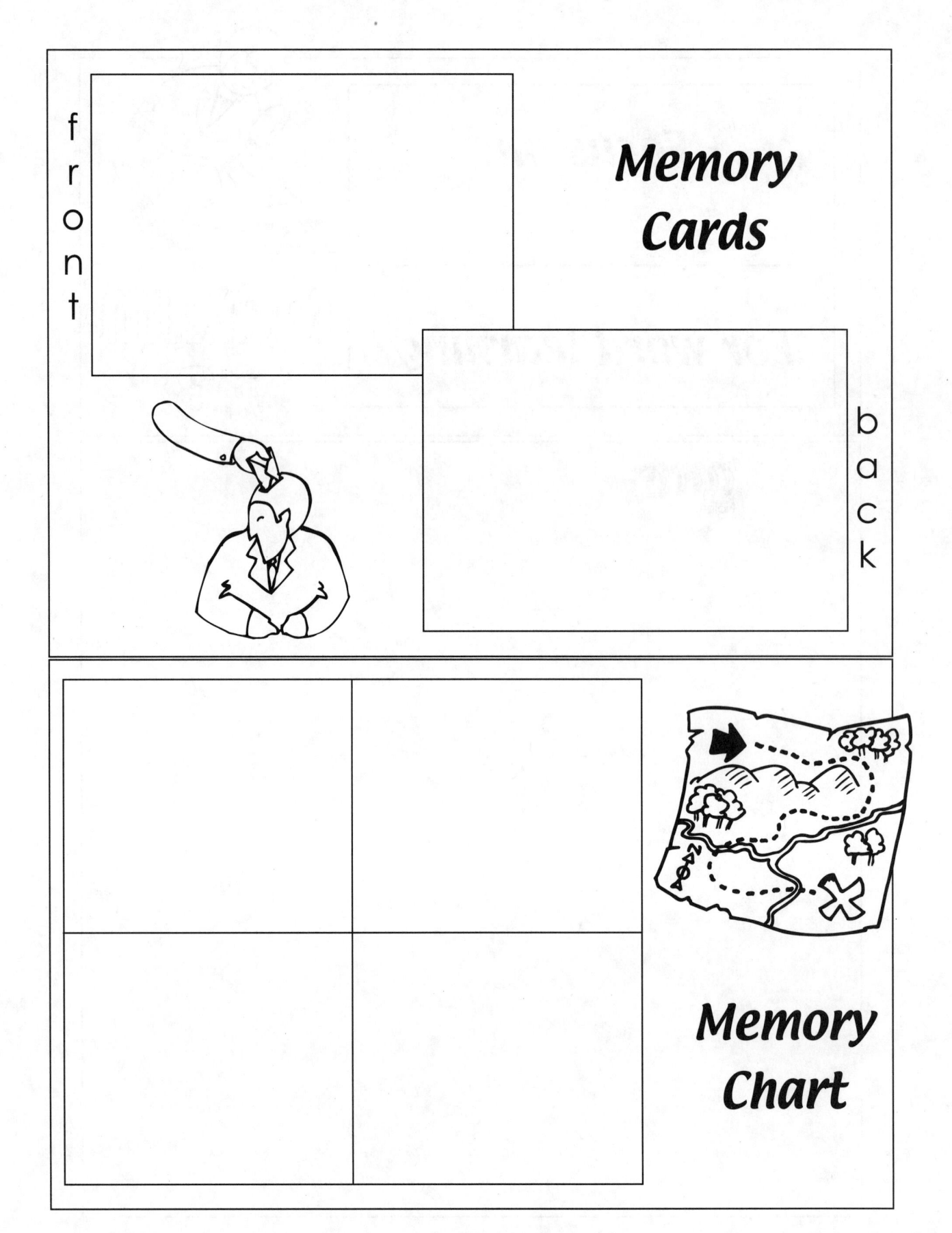

Memory Cards

back

Memory Chart

96

Strategy-at-a-Glance

Strategy: *Memory Cards*

Description: A word study procedure using personalized student-created cards that combine print and picture as a means to review words for reading and writing practice.

Step-By-Step:

1. Memory cards can be used for word recognition, vocabulary or spelling practice to promote long-term memory. Because children create a personal visual for each word, words can include those more abstract in nature, such as high frequency words *(was, they)*. The only materials needed are index cards and crayons or colored pencils.

2. One index card will be needed for each word, generally 4 x 6 or 5 x 7 inch cards. It is recommended that words are limited to five per week, allowing children to spend more time thinking about, creating and practicing each word, thereby intensifying learning through increased repetition.

3. The child writes the word on one side of the card, clearly printing it in a bright color for emphasis. High frequency words are written in one color so the word is seen as a whole, although a chunk may be color-coded in red to draw attention to the concept being learned (**b**at). For younger children, it may be helpful for the teacher to provide a good visual model with carefully spaced and well formed letters.

4. The child then creates a personal drawing on the other side of the card as a visual reminder for independent or peer practice. Encourage students to place a great deal of thought into creating a picture that will be easy to remember, as only one side of the card is used at a time. The initial picture should be created independently, providing time for sharing after the drawing is completed. This will reinforce the word while providing time to verbalize the thinking that went into creating drawings.

5. When cards are completed, they will be used for practice and review. For reading practice, cards are placed with the word in view so children can read the word and use the picture on the back to check for accuracy. For spelling practice, children use the picture side, turning the card over to check spelling after writing. This provides independent practice while emphasizing the reciprocal nature of reading and writing.

6. Provide time for brief daily practice sessions, generally limited to five minutes. One or two days a week, practice may include previous cards for continued learning. Memory cards are an excellent peer collaboration activity, as pictures provide a built in self-checking system to aid the partner in reading words independently. This also alleviates the need for the partner to be able to read the word, using the picture as an added resource.

Strategy-at-a-Glance

Strategy: *Memory Chart*

Description: A vocabulary and spelling review strategy providing a variety of information in recorded form in order to explore words at a deeper level.

Step-By-Step:

1. Memory Chart is designed as a review and extension strategy, so charts are completed after an initial learning activity to provide a general knowledge of the word selected. The learning may come from any meaningful context such as a story or word study. The cards provide a recorded form to explore the word in greater detail.

2. Create the chart by folding a piece of paper into four sections, with each section used for a different component. One memory chart is completed weekly as each word serves as a springboard to new ones to place emphasis on exploring interrelationships between words over rote memorization. An alternative is to identify five words to be divided among small groups of students. This will add a peer collaboration component and time for students to teach words to others. In this case, words may be related to a topic or story.

3. The first box in the top left corner is used to record the word clearly in print, providing a good visual for coding the word into long-term memory.

4. The top right corner includes known related words. This critical link to new word learning may include synonyms (***lethargic***: *tired, exhausted* or *weary*), common spelling patterns (**at**: *fat, cat, sat*) or other forms of a word (***happy***: *happiness, happily, unhappy*).

5. The box in the bottom left corner is used to create a unique and personalized representation of the word that will aid in remembering it. This may include a visual, acronym, drawing, cartoon, poem or rhyme. Children should create their own device to make it more personally relevant. This can be easily adapted for spelling by creating a "trick" to make the word more memorable (A principal is your *pal*.).

6. The final box in the bottom right corner is used to make a personal connection by stating an example or relating the word to a personal experience. This can be a sample taken directly from a story or from real life, serving to connect known to new learning.

7. Memory Charts can now be shared in pairs or small groups, as students explore word meanings and verbalize the thinking involved in creating charts. This sharing is a rich source for both review and new learning, particularly when it is repeated with several partners. New learning can be added in a different color to distinguish it from the initial study. If group words were selected, time is then provided for teaching words to peers.

Memory Chart Planning Form

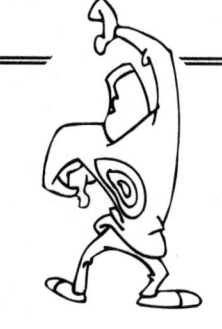

The word I want to learn is _____

These are related words

_____   _____

_____   _____

_____   _____

My personal connection to remember this word is

_____

_____

_____

My Picture

Reflective Pause #3

Do you provide instructional opportunities to teach children how to more effectively learn words for long-term recall?

Reinforced Current learning	Stimulated New learning

Explore

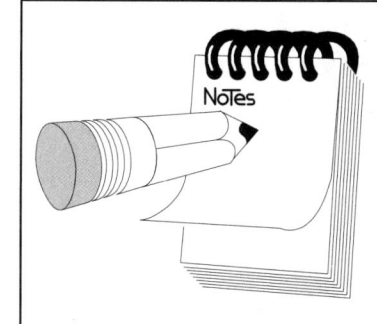

_____

&

_____

Maxim #4

Word Learning Patterns

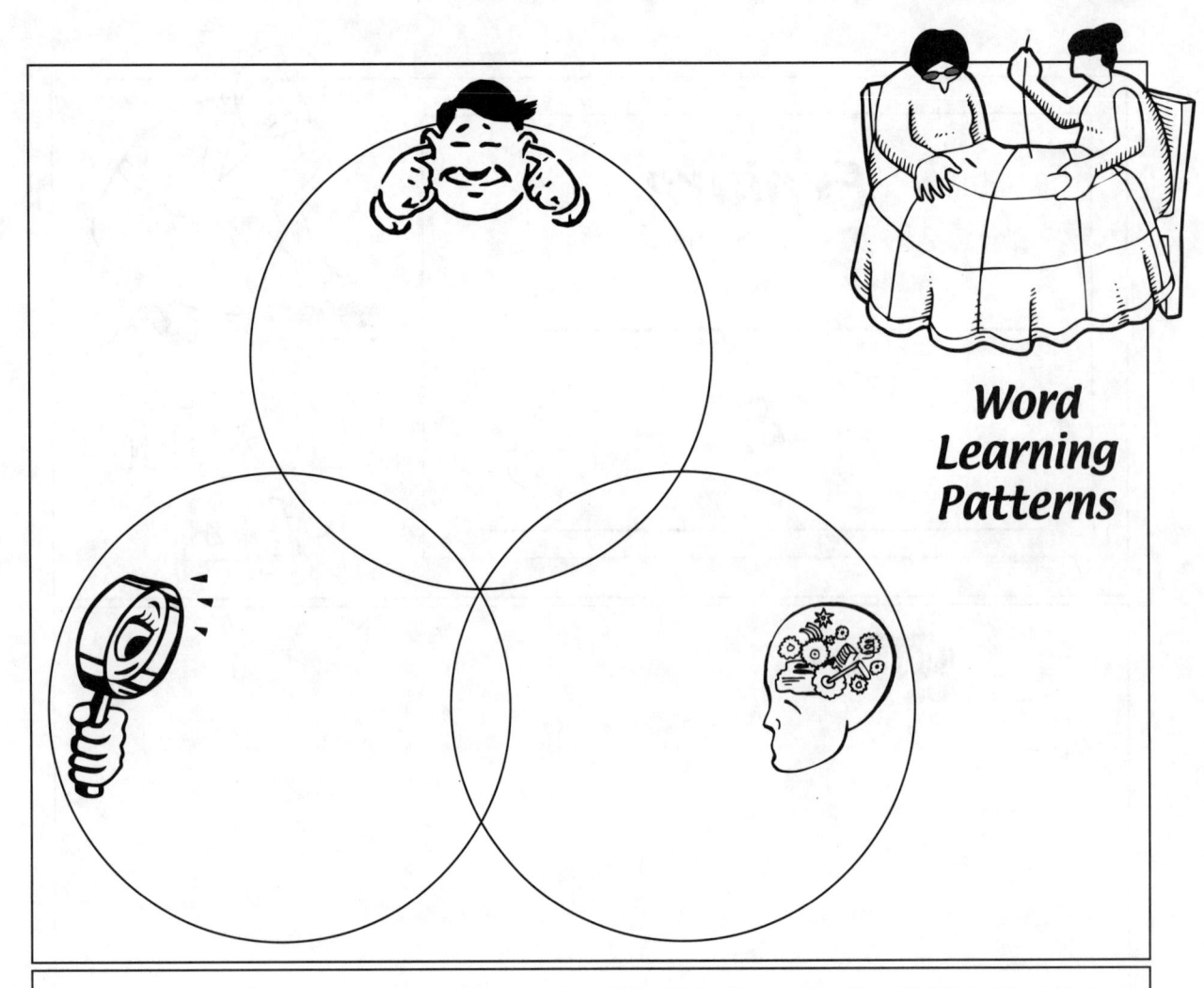

Common Onsets & Rimes

-ack	-ay	-ink
-ail	-eat	-ip
-ain	-ell	-it
-ake	-est	-ock
-ale	-ice	-oke
-ame	-ick	-op
-an	-ide	-ore
-ank	-ight	-ot
-ap	-ill	-uck
-ash	-in	-ug
-at	-ine	-ump
-ate	-ing	-unk
-aw	-ide	

Wylie & Durrell (1970)

Ways To Categorize Words

- initial letter (*boy, bear*)
- final letter (*cat; get*)
- common pattern (*fat, cat, sat*)
- prefix (*unhappy, unable*)
- suffix (*sickly, friendly*)
- word ending (*playing, going*)
- plural (*boys, cars*)
- irregular plural (*children, men*)
- proper noun (*Sally, Texas*)
- use (*book, read*)
- meaning (*big, large*)
- part of speech (*run, play*)
- physical feature (*I, a*)
- word tense (*saw, ran*)
- word length (*back, from*)

Word Maker Cups

1

2

3

Strategy-at-a-Glance

Strategy: *Word Maker Cups*

Description: An inexpensive way to provide a manipulative for reading words with a common chunk to highlight patterns and relationships between words.

Step-By-Step:

1. Word maker cups are an excellent source for practicing words with a common rime. Several onsets (letter/s before the vowel in a one syllable word) are written on one cup with a rime (the vowel and what follows) written on a second cup. When several onsets (*b, ch, f, m*) are combined with a rime (-at), this results in rhyming words (*bat, chat, fat, mat*). Styrofoam cups are an easy and inexpensive way to practice this skill alone or with peers.

2. Two styrofoam cups will be needed for each pattern being reinforced. The larger cups with a wider lip will provide more room to write letters and word patterns, so these are recommended. On one cup, write the rime you want to focus on. This should be written in red to draw attention to the concept to be learned.

3. On a second cup, write several onsets that can combine with the rime to make a word, spacing them far enough apart so that the child can see and read the words they will be creating. These can be written in black or blue marker. Be sure that these are real words (*fat, cat*) rather than non words (*dat, gat*) when combined with the rime.

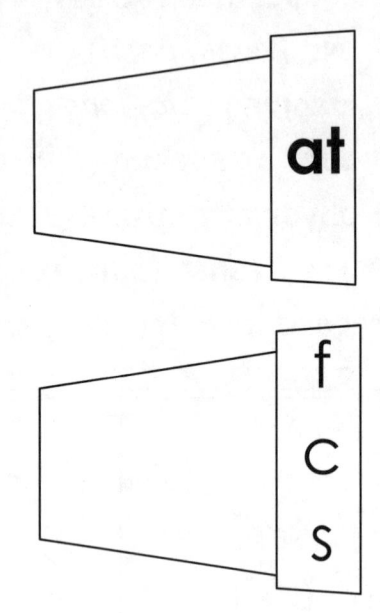

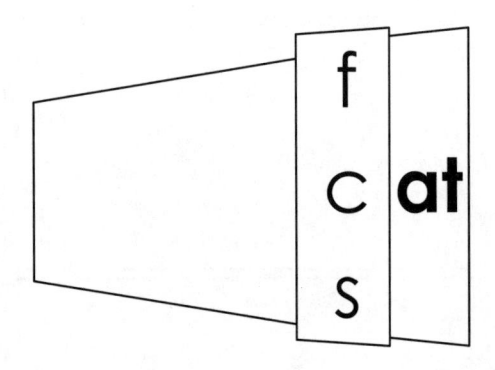

4. Place the rime cup inside the onset cup as shown. Notice that turning the outside cup so the onset is in line with the rime creates new words. By turning the cup slowly, the child continues to create more words that fit the rime, reading them aloud each time. Word maker cups can be adapted to include prefixes or suffixes, although it will be necessary to place a kleenex inside the outside cup so there is more room to write.

5. Cups can now be used for a literacy center activity or independent or buddy practice. New cups can easily be created to reinforce other word patterns as appropriate, providing a quick way to practice these concepts alone, with a peer or at home.

Reading Round Up

Step By Step

1.
2.
3.
4.
5.

Strategy-at-a-Glance

Strategy: *Reading Round Up*

Description: A word study strategy for collecting and organizing words that fit a specific pattern for the purpose of exploring the interrelationships that exist between words.

Step-By-Step:

1. Reading Round Up is a word study strategy designed to engage children in investigating and understanding relationships between words that fit a specific pattern. Relinquishing responsibility to students for collecting, investigating and analyzing words gives them a more active role in word learning. Focus is placed on developing a greater awareness of the written language system by using the *discovery approach* to make words more *memorable*. By closely inspecting a set of related words, children are able to make hypotheses about the relationships between words rather than merely citing arbitrary rules that frequently do not work. This serves as a valuable resource for unknown words and is more likely to transfer because students are active participants rather than passive recipients.

2. This strategy may follow a shared reading activity or mini-lesson, using sentences to reinforce learning and put this learning into practice. Begin by selecting a specific word study **focus** such as a chunk or spelling pattern, asking children to create a sentence using the target skill. If the target skill is *-ing ending*, for example, the sentence might be *My brother is playing football tonight*. The sentence allows words to begin in a meaningful context for repeated reading while the target word is used to address a specific skill. As appropriate, students may be asked to create two or three sentences to provide a larger word sample. Sentences will be written on sentence strips for rereading purposes, so be sure to check for spelling before recording sentences onto the strips (one-inch sentence strips can be purchased from Teaching Resource Center at www.trcabc.com). The target word should be color-coded or bolded as shown below to draw attention to the concept to be learned.

> I like runn**ing** outside with my brother.
>
> I am read**ing** a really great book.
>
> My mom is teach**ing** me to swim.

3. Sentence strips are now ready to be used as a **cut-up** sentence, cutting the words and punctuation apart so they can be rearranged and reread several times. This is a good time for the teacher to rotate among students to draw attention to key words or concepts and listen to students read.

| I | am | read**ing** | a | really | great | book | ! |

Reading Round Up: Continued

4. Once students have reassembled and reread sentences several times with a peer, provide time to **collaborate** in small groups of five to eight. This is an opportunity for children to explore existing patterns as a group before working with the teacher. Each member of the group will locate their target word, remove it from the sentence and place it in the center of the table. When related words are placed in full view, it becomes easier to notice patterns and relationships between them. Encourage students to carefully examine words and discuss how they are alike or different so they can be categorized in some way. The goal is to explore a pattern that will support future word learning. Words can be easily manipulated and rearranged as children make discoveries on their own before working with teacher support in the next stage. Again, this is a good time for the teacher to rotate, commenting on students' efforts to organize words. Avoid the temptation to take over, recognizing that the real power of learning comes from providing room for students to make their own discoveries. The teacher's role is merely to reinforce thinking and support students by actively engaging them in this process.

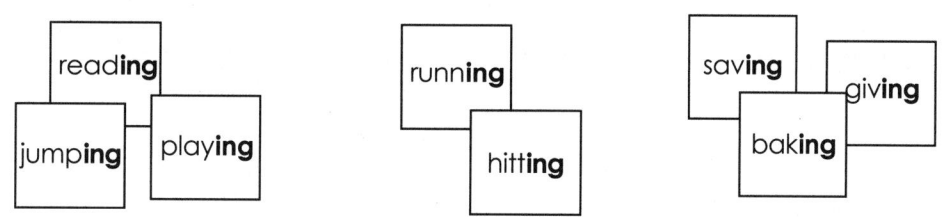

reading, jumping, playing

running, hitting

saving, giving, baking

5. Once words are categorized, bring students together to **organize** words in graphic form to highlight these relationships. Take a moment for each group to share group words and explain how and why they were categorized. Verbalizing this thinking is particularly important, using teacher questions and comments to guide and nurture thinking. As words are given, they can be written on individual index cards or transparency pieces so they are easier to manipulate as students suggest how to organize them. Reinforce thinking and draw attention to key points that may have gone unnoticed. After all words have been organized they can be placed on a chart or web as shown below. Engage children in selecting a label for each category that will *explain* the relationship. Again, keep in mind that the key is *explaining* words and relationships rather than citing rules.

+ing	drop e +ing	double letter +ing
playing	saving	putting
reading	giving	running
jumping	baking	hitting

6. **Elaborate** on learning over time by adding to the existing list, gradually placing new words on the chart in the appropriate location. In some cases, this may result in an additional category, such as exceptions. After two or three weeks, words can be transferred to a *Big Book of Word Patterns & Relationships*. This ongoing collection will result in a long-term resource that can be used and added to throughout the year.

Reading Round Up Planning Form

Word Study Focus

I am going to use this word to fit the focus

_____

This is my sentence using the focus word

_____

_____

Circle any words you are not sure are spelled correctly

This is my sentence with the correct spelling

_____

_____

These are other words I know that fit the focus

_____   _____

_____   _____

_____   _____

_____   _____

Reading Round Up Group Form

Word Study Focus

These are our group word study focus words

_____   _____

_____   _____

_____   _____

_____   _____

We think these words should be organized in this way

We think the pattern is _____

_____

©2004 by Dr. Mary Howard

Reflective Pause #4

Do you help students to see the relationships and patterns in words by drawing attention to these features on a daily basis?

Reinforced Current learning	Stimulated New learning

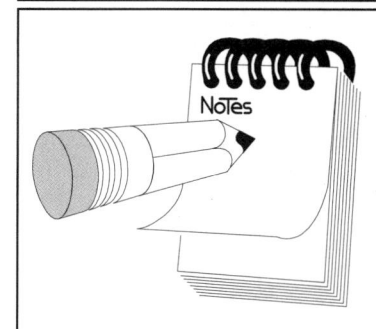

Emphasize
_____
Contexts

Maxim #5

Sentence a Day

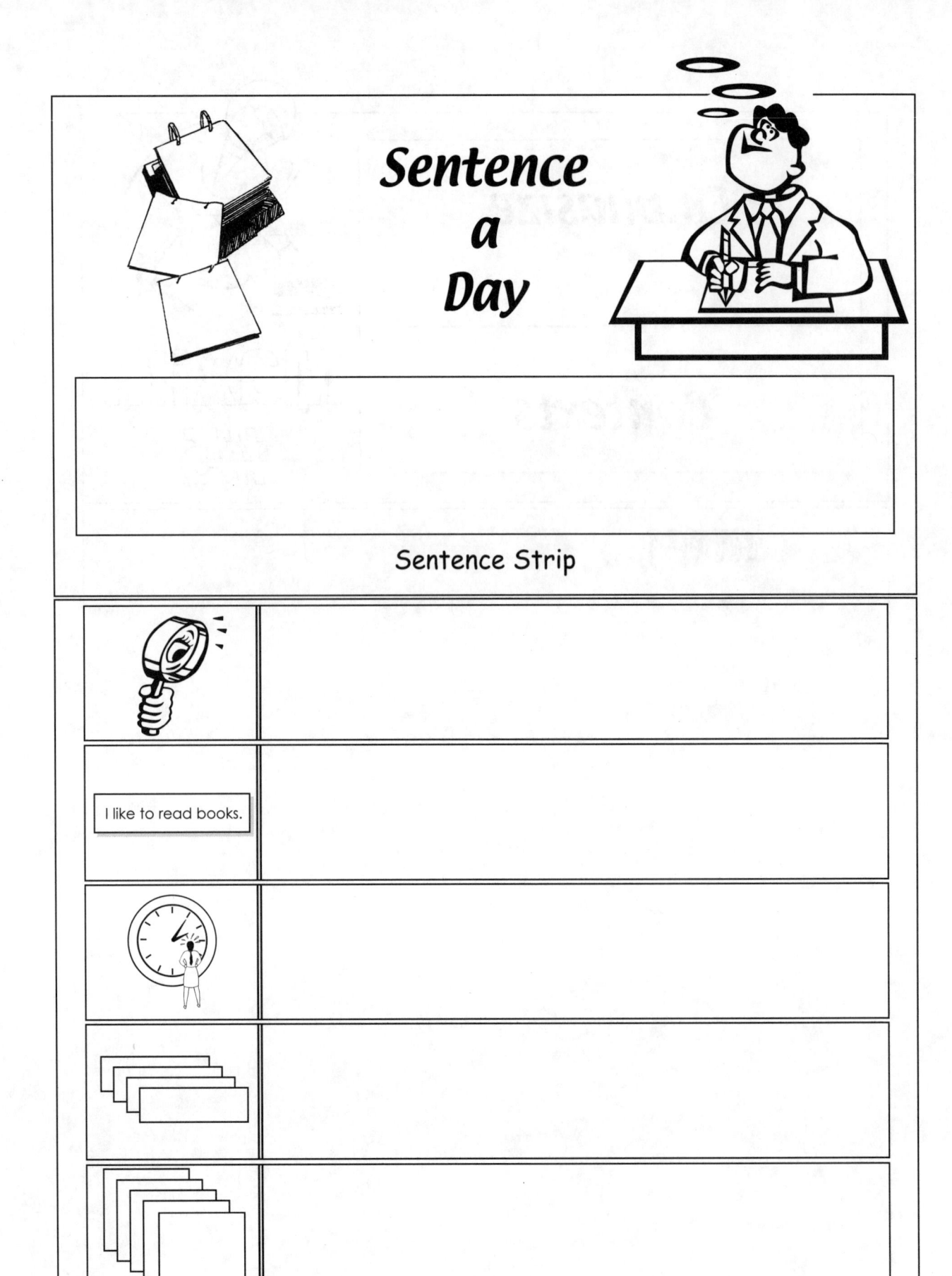

Sentence Strip

112

Strategy-at-a-Glance

Strategy: *Sentence a Day (Reading the Desk)*

Description: A strategy for initiating a daily student-generated sentence for reading, decoding, vocabulary, and spelling practice, using sentences to create a book version at the end of the week.

Step-By-Step:

1. **Select a focus** that will be used all week to generate sentences. This may be a starter to reinforce a high frequency word (*Something you like; can do*), topic (spiders, Columbus), spelling pattern (chunk, word ending), part of speech (adjective), punctuation (dialogue, comma) or general category (*About You, Things you Enjoy, Favorite Animals*). The focus is intended only to initiate and guide sentences so a book version can be created at the end of the week. This allows the teacher to highlight a specific teaching point while providing meaningful practice for reading. For younger students, the starter provides a repetitive, predictable print source (*I like to run; I like to play; I like to jump rope*). Sentences always come from the child, avoiding taking control once the focus has been suggested. If appropriate, have students create only one sentence on Monday that will be used all week. This will result in a class collaboration book at the end of the week.

2. Once the focus is selected, **generate and record** the sentences on strips. Beginning readers may dictate the sentence so that they can be recorded on the strips by the teacher, providing a legible print source that assures correct spelling, since all word *must* be spelled accurately. Students may also write the sentences on a piece of paper and find three peers to check for spelling, asking the teacher to make a final check before they are recorded on the strips. Strips are generally one by six inches so that five sentences will fit in the upper left corner of the desk as shown below. One inch sentence strips are available from Teaching Resource Center (www.trcabc.com) or strips can be cut from a manila folder. Sentences will be displayed on each child's desk for the entire week to read and review. A half sheet of a plastic report cover can be taped to the desk on three sides to protect the strips. This will also make it easy for sentences to be removed and replaced if the desk is used by multiple students.

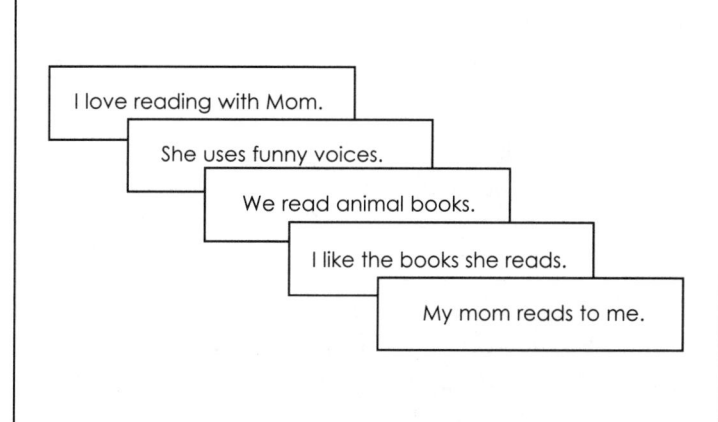

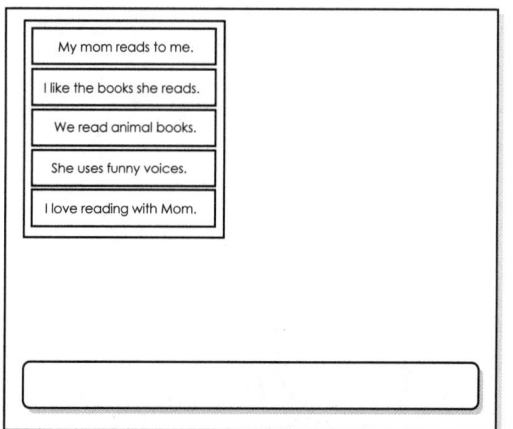

Reading the Desk: Continued

3. Once sentences are on the desk, **revisit and highlight** the print by providing time for children to read with a partner. Children are never asked to read any sentence other than their own unless they volunteer to do so. Words are reinforced through reading personal sentences to a partner and by listening to peers read so that known words are strengthened while providing *exposure* to new words. Encourage students to point to each word as they read to draw attention to the print. Take opportunities to reinforce sentences spontaneously throughout the day, particularly for children needing extra practice. This can be done easily by stopping briefly beside a desk and asking the child to locate a word in the sentence or to *read the desk*. Specific print features may also be addressed to build on word learning and sound awareness. Reinforce print concepts in the early stages *(find one/two letters/words; find the first/last letter/word, count the number of letters/words; point and read)*, gradually focusing on other print features by asking students to locate and frame them between their two index fingers:

- initial letter/cluster
- word ending
- part of speech
- letter combination
- spelling pattern
- final letter/s
- high frequency word
- word length
- rich language
- dialogue
- synonym
- antonym
- punctuation
- alphabet
- root word

4. **Add and connect** sentences as a new one is created each subsequent day, using the selected topic. Repeat the activities described, offering new opportunities such as finding words in combined sentences that are connected in some way (initial letter, adjectives, four-letter words, action words). Provide ample time to revisit sentences throughout the week, emphasizing specific points by highlighting key words, modeling fluency, and reinforcing concepts.

5. On Friday afternoon, sentences are removed from the desk to **combine and celebrate** in book form. Sentences can be rewritten or glued to the bottom of five pieces of paper. They are now ready for students to add illustrations, stapling them together for a personal book for rereading. If an individual sentence was used all week, children can complete a weekly journal page as well as to create a class version by combining all sentences into a single book (*Things We Like; Our Spider Facts*).

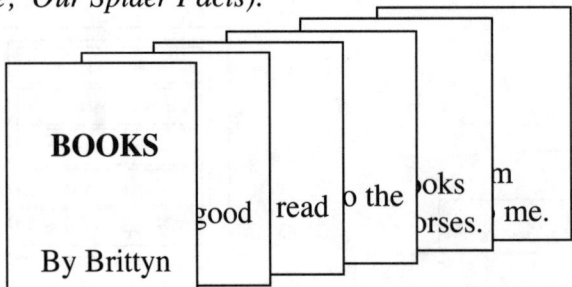

6. Some children will benefit from additional experiences with the sentence. This may include creating a cut-up sentence to reassemble and read or extending learning at home or with a partner as described on the following pages. These opportunities will not be needed for every child, but should always be an option for children needing additional support.

Sample Parent Letter: Sentence-a-Day

Dear Parents,

This year your child will participate in a weekly activity called *Sentence a Day*. A topic will be selected at the beginning of each week. Your child will use the topic to create a new sentence daily that will be used for a variety of reading and spelling activities. These sentences will be combined for an illustrated book at the end of the week. The sentences will reinforce what your child already knows and pave the way for new learning. You can support my efforts in many ways by using the sentences at home.

Your child will bring home a new sentence on a sentence strip each day. Please find a special place to display the sentence, such as the front of the refrigerator, a door, wall or filing cabinet. Tape new sentences under the previous ones. You might create a sentence of your own to provide a good model and display it beside your child's. Print words clearly with correct spelling, letting your child watch as you write. Talk about each word, focusing on specific letters as appropriate.

Take turns reading the sentences daily, pointing to each word and encouraging your child to do the same. After reading, you may draw attention to words or letters (see attached list of ideas), using encouraging language (*My first word is* the. *What is your first word?; I have five words in my sentence. How many words do you have?; I have a word that starts with the letter* b *{basket}. What word do you have?; Show me _____; What is your fifth word? Which word is capitalized?*). Be creative and playful, challenging your child to find and read words.

At the end of the week, rewrite the sentences or glue the strips to the bottom of five pieces of paper. The pages are now ready to be illustrated and stapled together in sequence as a personal book for rereading. Please store the books in a special place so your child can reread them as new books are added. Thank you for participating in this wonderful shared reading activity. By reinforcing my efforts at home, we can make this a year of joy and learning for your child!

Suggestions To Reinforce Sentence-a-Day

- Specific word/letter
- Word order (third, fifth)
- Upper/lower case letters
- First letter/word
- Last letter/word
- Capital/lowercase letter
- Related words (same/opposite)
- Vocabulary meaning
- Same initial/final letter
- Spelling pattern (fat, cat)
- Punctuation
- Describing word
- Part of speech
- High frequency word
- Number of words/letters
- Letter combination
- Longest/shortest word

Displaying Sentences

Refrigerator

- I like books.
- Mom reads to me.
- I love my mom.
- I like her to read.
- We love to read.
- I am Mary's Mom.
- I love Mary.
- I read to her.
- She likes to read.
- We love books.

manila folder

- I like reading to Mom.
- She helps me read every day.
- She tells me I am a good reader.
- We make a book together.
- We love to read our books.
- I like being Mary's Mom.
- I like reading to Mary.
- We read our sentences together.
- It's fun to make new sentences.
- Mary is my favorite reader.

©2004 by Dr. Mary Howard

Sample Sentence Buddy Letter: Sentence-a-Day

Dear Sentence Buddy,

Thank you for volunteering to help me in my classroom this year. You have been specially recommended by your teacher and you should be proud of this honor. As a Sentence Buddy, you will write a sentence each day to share with your buddy and listen to your buddy read their sentence. I will let you know what the topic is at the beginning of each week. When you come to my classroom, bring your new sentence with you, making sure it is nicely printed on the sentence strip with all the words checked for spelling. Ask your teacher to check your sentence before you come to my class.

Add your sentence to the Buddy Reading Folder. You will have ten minutes to complete one or two activities of your choice. Leave the Buddy Folder in the basket each day so it will be ready to use the next day.

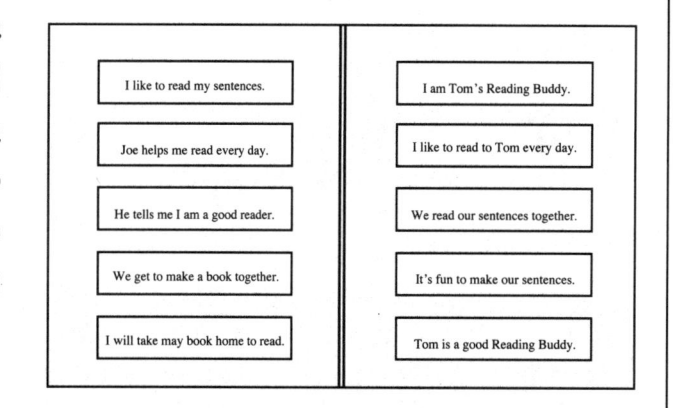

I like to read my sentences.	I am Tom's Reading Buddy.
Joe helps me read every day.	I like to read to Tom every day.
He tells me I am a good reader.	We read our sentences together.
We get to make a book together.	It's fun to make our sentences.
I will take may book home to read.	Tom is a good Reading Buddy.

You will spend about twenty minutes in my classroom every Friday to create a book using the sentences you each wrote during the week. Everything you need will be in the center. Write or tape sentences on each page so they can be illustrated. Reread the books one or two times and place them in the Buddy Folder before you leave so you can read them again on Monday.

Thank you for being a Sentence Buddy this year. This is a wonderful way to support your buddy in learning new words. Your buddy is lucky to have such a capable and responsible reader to share in this activity. I am very pleased to have your help and look forward to having you in my room this year. Please let me know if you have any questions.

Sentence Buddy Tutoring Guide

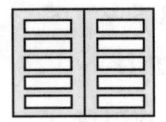

1. Bring your sentence to class every day and put it in the Buddy Folder. Be sure it is clearly printed and that every word is spelled correctly. Come a few minutes early to look at your buddy's sentence.

2. Set the timer for ten minutes (twenty minutes on Friday). Select one or two activities you would like to do each day. Be sure to mark them on the Response Form, writing any words that you worked on.

3. Take turns reading and rereading the sentence, listening to your buddy read to you and reading your sentence to your buddy. Never ask your buddy to read your sentence unless your buddy makes that choice.

4. Compare the sentences by using yours as a model. (*I have a word that starts with B: bicycle. What word do you have that starts with b?; I have a capital H. Do you have a small h?; My first word is _____. What is your first word?*). Ask your buddy to find words (*Show me _____. Where is the word like?*). This will give you a chance to work on specific words.

5. Magnetic letters are in the center to *make and break* one word in your buddy's sentence. Your buddy will put the letters in the correct order, mix them up and make the word again. Ask your buddy to point and slide one finger under the word while reading.

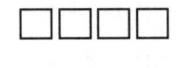

6. Print your buddy's sentence carefully on a strip. Cut up each word as your buddy watches so that your buddy can then put the words back together in the correct order to reread. Mix it up to make the sentence again several times.

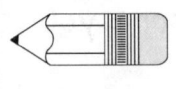

7. Ask your buddy to choose one word in the sentence to write from memory. Remind your buddy to look at the word and then cover the word before writing it without looking at it. Check the spelling and repeat this several times.

8. On Friday, the sentences will be used to make a book. Tape or write each sentence to the bottom of a page. Illustrate pages and staple them together to make a book. Reread before you leave and place the books back in the folder.

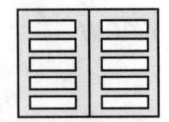

9. When you finish each day, your buddy will help you clean up. Put the Response Form and books in the Buddy Folder and leave it in the basket.

©2004 by Dr. Mary Howard

Sentence Buddy Response Form

Buddy _____ Tutor _____

	Monday	Tuesday	Wednesday	Thursday	Friday
👄					
👁					
✋					
▯▯▯					
✏️					
🗂					

©2004 by Dr. Mary Howard

Strategy-at-a-Glance

Strategy: *Connected Sentences*

Description: A strategy for creating meaningful sentences to reinforce high frequency words independently and with a partner.

Step-By-Step:

1. You will need small squares of blank paper. These can be created by cutting pieces of construction paper or by cutting small index cards in half. This activity may occur in close proximity to the word wall or other print resource, such as a spelling or word list. A dictionary, spell check or independent reading selection can also be used as a support.

2. Children are asked to select and write individual words on each piece of paper to create a sentence, reminding them to check spelling. A simple drawing may also be used to represent unknown words. Writing words on individual pieces will make it easy to add, rearrange, substitute and omit words to create just the right sentence. It will also make it easier to work with a buddy to create new sentences as discussed below.

| I | like | to | play | ⚾ | with | my | ☺ | ! |

3. When children are satisfied with their sentence, the pieces can be glued or recopied onto a piece of paper so the sentence can be illustrated. A Sentence Journal may be created for this purpose, using blank pages stapled or bound together horizontally. This will provide a long-term resource for reading and writing as each new sentence is added as well as time to self-select and reread sentences throughout the year. This is particularly important for students who do not have a growing store of sight vocabulary.

4. Turn the activity into a collaborative task by creating Buddy Sentences, using the sentences each child creates individually to share with a buddy. Buddies can combine and rearrange words to create new sentences using several guidelines:

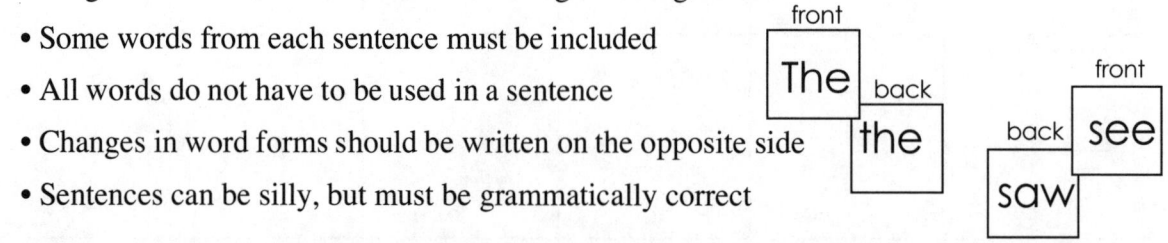

- Some words from each sentence must be included
- All words do not have to be used in a sentence
- Changes in word forms should be written on the opposite side
- Sentences can be silly, but must be grammatically correct

5. An optional form is provided on the following page to record each child's initial sentence, with spaces for the combined sentences beneath it. This activity promotes independence as well as collaborative skills that promotes new learning. Working together allows students to spend a little more time with the initial words and to continue learning as new words are added. Recording sentences on the form also gives the teacher a way to check words and the grammatical structure of sentences.

Buddy Sentence Form

Buddy #1	Sentence #1

Buddy #2	Sentence #2

Combined Buddy Sentences

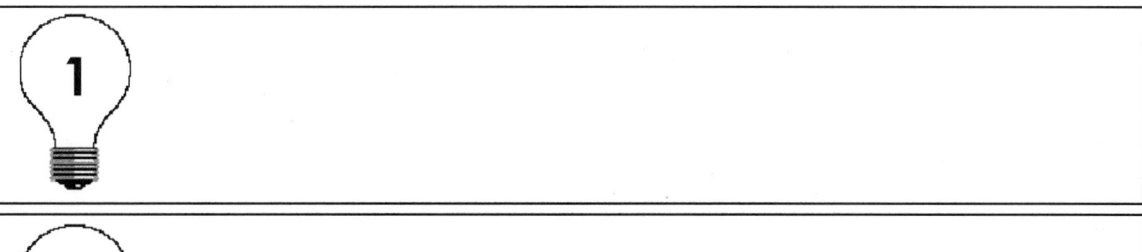

1

2

3

4

©2004 by Dr. Mary Howard

Reflective Pause #5

Do you focus word learning activities on daily experiences that emphasize wide reading and wide writing?

Reinforced Current learning	Stimulated New learning

Celebrate the _____

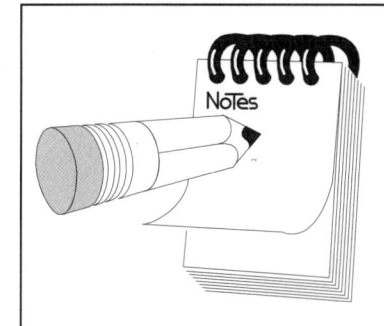

Maxim #6

123

Personal Partner Pockets

Rhyming words	Story words
Word endings	Content area
Prefixes	High frequency
Suffixes	Vocabulary
New word forms	Related Words
My Pattern Words	**My Sight Words**

Guidelines

1
2
3
4
5

Strategy-at-a-Glance

Strategy: *Personal Partner Pockets*

Description: A daily peer collaboration activity for selecting, sharing and practicing self-selected words to study a specific pattern and reinforce sight vocabulary.

Step-By-Step:

1. A two-pocket folder will be needed for this strategy. Each pocket will be used to house word cards, with the left pocket holding words that fit a specific pattern and the right pocket for sight vocabulary. Label each pocket as shown.

My Pattern Words	My Sight Words

2. Self-selected words are a powerful source of word learning due to an increase in motivation for learning. This can have a tremendous impact on recall. Children will select three to five words they *want* to learn that fit each category, limiting the number so the focus is on long-term memory. This generally begins as a whole class activity, providing time for students to select and share words after the initial learning. Pattern words reflect a specific concept *(-at words; words that end with -ing; words with the prefix un-; words that come from the root word like)*. Sight word cards are those that the child wants to read and write instantly. Words can come from personal sources or may be selected from a specific story or topic. The teacher may also designate a category *(Select words that mean big.; Find adjectives that describe the character in the story.)*. Children create a card for each word by writing it in large print on the front, with patterns color-coded as appropriate. A picture or photo may be added on the back as a visual to support learning.

3. After children have created the cards, provide time for them to share with multiple partners. Use only one pocket at a time so attention is focused on limited learning in five minute blocks. Time may be provided later in the day to share words in the second pocket. Students will take turns reading words to a partner before moving on to a new one. This will provide ample repetition while offering exposure to new words from each partner.

4. After sharing, discuss and list any words that fit a category or pattern. Words may be organized on a chart, web or graph, engaging students in this process to provide a long-term resource resulting from this shared reading activity.

5. This is a valuable procedure to repeat first thing in the morning and at the end of the day, providing a quick and energetic way to practice words. Combining self-selection and collaboration will maximize word learning in a pleasurable way.

Pattern

My Pattern Words

I shared these pattern words *with* my partners

_____   _____

_____   _____

_____

I learned these pattern words *from* my partners

_____   _____

_____   _____

_____   _____

I found more pattern words I want to include

_____   _____   _____

_____   _____   _____

_____   _____   _____

©2004 by Dr. Mary Howard

Story or Category	My Sight Words

I want to learn to read and write these words instantly

_____   _____

_____   _____

_____

I selected these words because

_____

_____

I plan to learn these words by

- _____
- _____
- _____
- _____

(Circle any words you think you need to repeat next week)

©2004 by Dr. Mary Howard

Living Posters

Step By Step

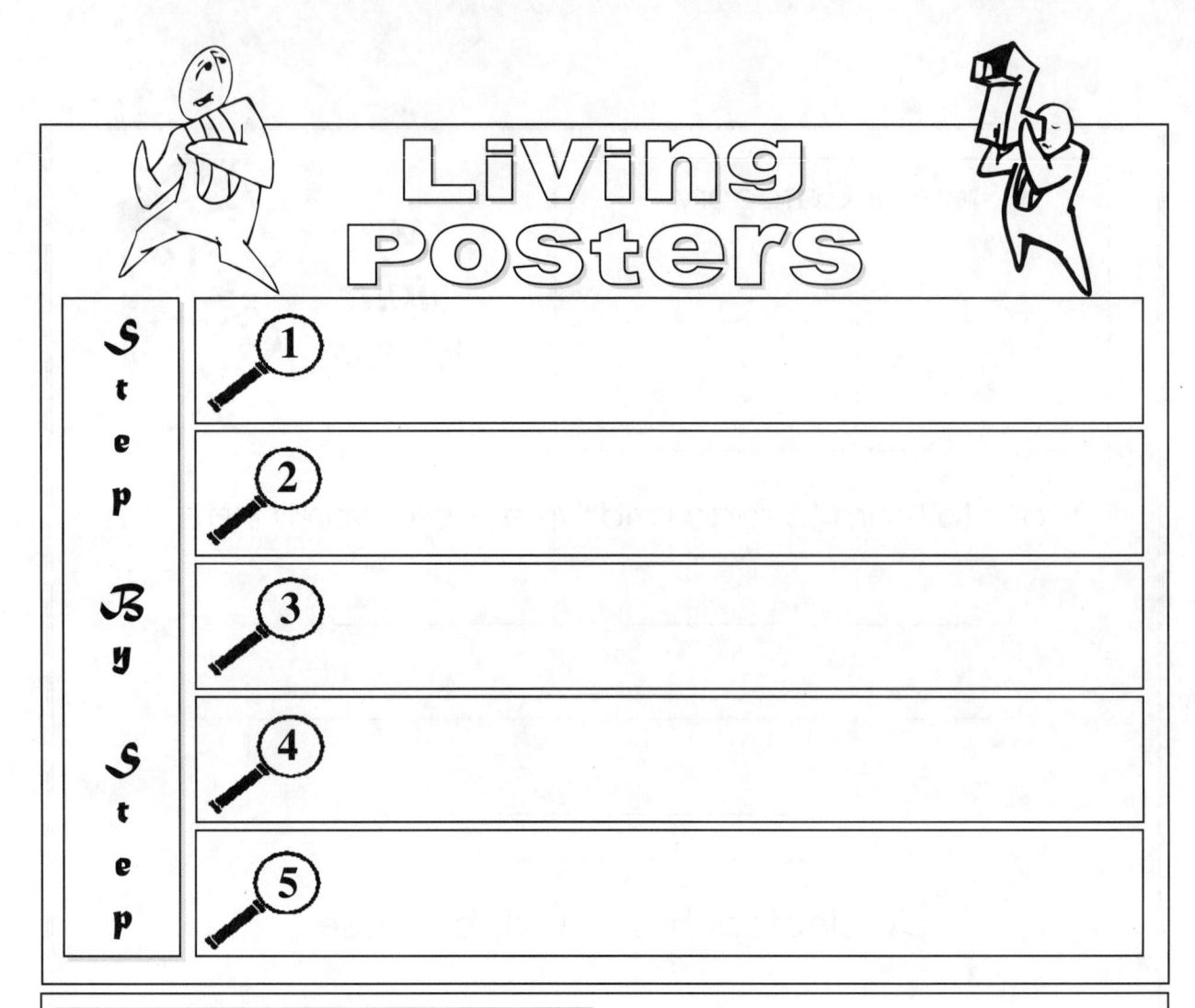

1.
2.
3.
4.
5.

The Possibilities

Alphabet recognition
Sound/symbol relationships
Spelling patterns
Prefixes and suffixes
Vocabulary
Related words
Parts of speech
Content words
Character attributes
Story components

Strategy-at-a-Glance

Strategy: *Living Posters*

Description: Using photographs to create a concrete visual hook for words, sounds and concepts by engaging students in selecting, designing and posing for recorded forms.

Step-By-Step:

1. Begin by identifying the concept you want to reinforce. This may be letters of the alphabet, a phonics concept or words from a story or specific area of study. Posters will be used all year long to reinforce learning, displaying them in place of commercial charts and posters. Each poster should be on an 8 1/2" by 11" piece of cardstock that can be laminated for continued use. This will make it last and will result in a form easy to store in a ring binder for personal study and review.

2. Briefly review the concept you have selected and initiate several examples. This may be a brief review of previous learning, a mini-lesson that follows a vocabulary lesson or shared reading activity using a big book, song or poem.

3. After the learning activity, tell students you are going to create a living poster. Identify the focus and ask them to think about an action word that can be photographed. It is important that students are engaged in selecting the key word to represent the concept. If the *-ing* chunk is the focus, children may select the word *sing* as the target word, or a word that will represent the concept. One or more students can then act out the word so a photograph can be taken as a visual representation. Digital cameras have simplified this process and will make it easy to add, modify or create multiple samples for comparison as an ongoing project.

4. Write the word at the bottom of the poster in large easy-to-read letters and glue the photograph to the top. The word or concept being reinforced can be color-coded in red (s**ing**; **b**aby; **un**happy) to draw attention to these features. Laminate posters to display them on the wall or collect them in a ring binder. This ongoing reference serves as a framework for teaching analogies (*How can this word help you spell the word **bring**?*) and offers springboards to new words (*What other words mean the same thing?*). Posters can be used to highlight related words and to extend word learning by focusing attention on the relationships and patterns that make print more dependable.

5. Use posters all year for instructional opportunities and encourage students to use these references by drawing attention to words during reading and writing activities (*Do you see a word that will help you?*). Add new posters throughout the year and revisit them frequently to connect known to new. Involve students in modifying, rearranging and adding posters to support new learning. The posters are used in place of commercial products because engaging students in creating them is a powerful addition, so take advantage of these opportunities.

Reflective Pause #6

Do you celebrate word learning through experiences that allow children to play with words and language?

Reinforced Current learning	Stimulated New learning

Taking a TRIP Down Memory Lane

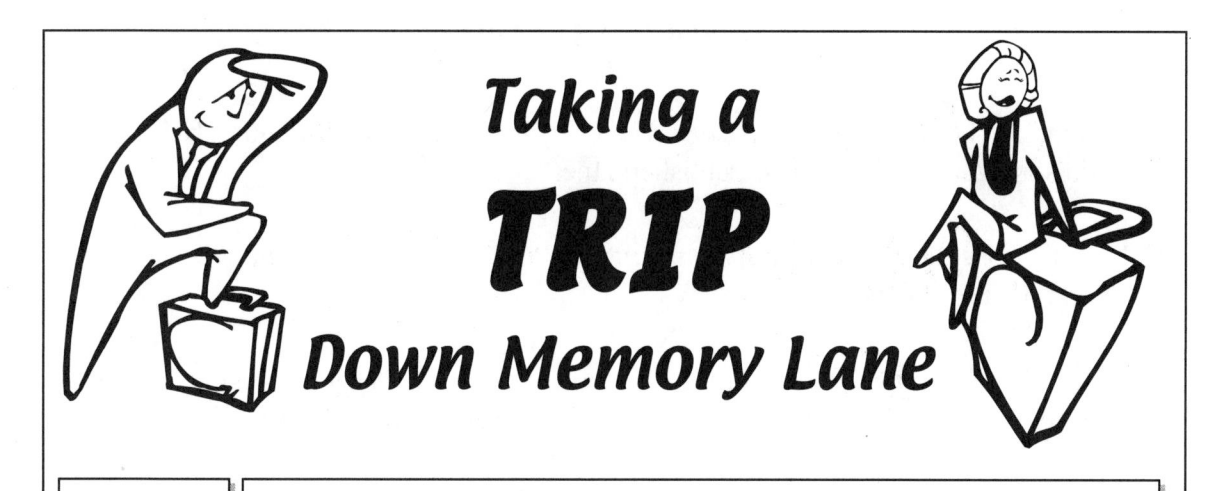

T

I want to **T**ry this tomorrow

R

This **R**einforced my knowledge

I

Something **I**nteresting I learned

P

I make a **P**romise to change this

RESOURCES CITED

Allington, R. L (2001). *What Really Matters for Struggling Readers.* New York: Addison-Wesley Educational Publishers, Inc.

Caldwell, J. S. (2002). *Reading Assessment: A Primer for Teachers and Tutors.* New York: Guilford Press.

Clay, M. M. & Imlach, R. H. (1971). Juncture, pitch & stress as reading behavior variables. *Journal of Verbal Learning and Verbal Behavior,* 10, 133-139.

Cunningham, P. M. (1980). Teaching Were, With, What, and Other "Four-Letter Words. *The Reading Teacher,* 34, 160-163

Durkin, D. (1983). *Reading comprehension instruction: What the research says.* Presentation at the first annual Tarleton State University Reading Conference, Stephenville, TX.

Krashen, S. (1993). *The Power of Reading.* CT*:* Libraries Unlimited, Inc.

Leslie, L. & Caldwell, J. (2001). *The Qualitative Reading Inventory 3.* New York: Addison Wesley Longman.

Ohlhausen, M. & Jepsen, M. (1992). Lessons from Goldilocks: 'Somebody's been choosing my books but I can make my own choices now!' *The New Advocate,* 5, 31-46.

Pinnell, G. S.; Pikulski, J. J.; Wixson, K. K.; Campbell, J. R.; Gough, P. B. & Beatty, A. S. (1995) Listening to children read aloud. Washington DC: U.S. Department of Education, National Center for Educational Statistics.

Rasinski, T. V. (2000). Speed does matter in reading. *The Reading Teacher,* 54 (2), 146-151.

Tate, M. L. (2003). *Worksheets Don't Grow Dendrites.* CA: Corwin Press.

Siegel, M. (1983). *Reading as signification.* Unpublished doctoral dissertation, Indiana University: Bloomington.

Wylie, R. E. & Durrell, D. D. (1970). Teaching vowels through phonograms. *Elementary English,* 47, 787-791.

Key Points

Bright Ideas
I want to remember

I can make these changes tomorrow

Key Points

Bright Ideas I want to remember

I can make these changes tomorrow

©2004 by Dr. Mary Howard

Key Points

**Bright Ideas
I want to remember**

I can make these changes tomorrow

Key Points

Bright Ideas I want to remember

I can make these changes tomorrow

©2004 by Dr. Mary Howard

Key Points

Bright Ideas I want to remember

I can make these changes tomorrow

©2004 by Dr. Mary Howard

Key Points

Bright Ideas I want to remember

I can make these changes tomorrow

My Teacher Thinks I'm Special!
©1992 Dr. Mary Howard

My teacher thinks I'm special.
It comes as no surprise.
She doesn't have to say so;
I see it in her eyes.

She tells me all about herself,
Her family, friends, and dreams.
That makes me feel important.
She trusts me with those things.

She says I have potential.
She sees things others don't.
She sees the things that I *will* do,
And not the things I *won't*.

She puts her hand on top of mine
And tells me, "Way to go!"
"You can do it!" "Try again!"
"I'm proud of you, you know."

It's not my fault; it's really not.
There's three ways to spell "to."
With choices always facing me,
I don't know what to do.

Sometimes I can't spell anything;
My fives are upside down.
Two plus two makes three, I think.
I turn *b* and *d* around.

The rules all have exceptions.
You can't depend on those.
The letters can say anything.
What is that word? Who knows!

I guess that when you've learned to read
It's easy to forget
That reading is quite difficult
When you haven't learned how yet!

My teacher tells me stories,
Sets the words and pictures free.
And while I'm learning how to read,
Such tales she shares with me.

My teacher takes my hand in hers
And guides me on the way.
She knows I'll read in my own time...
Just maybe not today!

My teacher thinks I'm special,
Unique and very bright.
A shining star in my own way...
Know what? I *know* she's right!

drmaryhoward.com
mhoward@drmaryhoward.com
Reading Connections
PO Box 52426
Tulsa, OK 74152-0426
(918) 744-8698

Bring **Mary** to your school

Dr. Mary Howard is an internationally renowned expert, leader and change-agent in the field of literacy. A powerhouse consultant and dynamic speaker, Mary has worked with countless educators to create literacy programs grounded in current brain research. She is often described as a "teachers' teacher," gifted with a special insight into classroom realities and a master at translating research into practice.

An educator for over three decades, Mary brings to the table extensive classroom experience as a grade 1-6 special educator, grade K-12 reading tutor, reading specialist and Reading Recovery® teacher. Years as a consultant, university instructor, professional storyteller, author and nationwide lecturer have further expanded the wealth of knowledge she has to share. Whether speaking or consulting, Mary's prime conviction is to help educators create lifelong learners.

Fast-paced and inspiring, Dr. Howard's seminars are packed with dozens of engaging strategies that can be immediately implemented into any curriculum. Her no-nonsense approach gives teachers a deeper understanding of the learning process, enabling them to transform the teaching process into a powerful tool for maximizing the potential of *every* child.

Turning Struggles into Successes
As quick fixes and teaching to the test continue to take a stronghold, few suffer more than struggling readers, whose unique learning needs have long been ignored by conventional programs and generic recipes. In this eye-opening seminar you will explore the most critical aspects of literacy. Even more importantly, you will receive easy to implement strategies for effecting real change.

Enhancing Comprehension for Struggling Readers
It is impossible to underestimate the role comprehension plays in the reading process. The true value of words on a page is derived through the meaning they deliver. This informative seminar provides a "treasure chest" of strategies to engage students and maximize meaning throughout reading. Discover the secrets of teaching strategies students will use for a lifetime.

Implementing an Effective Guided Reading Program
Guided reading is a powerful tool for intensifying instruction in small groups. Flexible temporary homogeneous groups allow teachers to offer students individualized support through carefully selected texts. With warmth and wisdom, Mary shows how to provide rich opportunities for reinforcing current knowledge while teaching new strategies in powerful ways.

Creating an Exemplary Literacy Program
To create rich literacy contexts, schools must first establish criteria for working toward that goal. This inspiring presentation discusses ten maxims for designing exemplary literacy environments and the essential principles that support teachers in this process. Learn highly engaging strategies that will turn you into a powerful change agent in the classroom.

Building a Rich Reading and Writing Vocabulary
Daily interactions with language and print offer priceless opportunities to expand vocabulary. Learn how to implement proven techniques that promote long-term memory using collaboration, movement, color and mnemonic devices. Discover strategies for continuous, lifelong word learning in this energizing session,.

Building Powerful Frameworks for Discussions
The ultimate goal of education is to build environments that nurture literate lives. This can be accomplished by immersing students in a multitude of real-life reading experiences. This session highlights dynamic frameworks for celebrating meaningful print throughout the day. Learn to create engaging opportunities for interacting with texts across the curriculum.

141

$89.95 Book with Audio Seminar
$399.95 Book with DVD Seminar

New from Dr. Mary Howard

ORDER FORM
Please include your phone number in case there are questions regarding your order.

Qty	ISBN	Title	Unit Price	Total
	0-9742877-1-7	Turning Struggles into Successes – Book/Audio Seminar Quantity Discounts: 2-4 (10%), 5-9 (20%), 10-14 (30%), 15+ (40%)	$89.95	
	0-9742877-2-5	Turning Struggles into Successes – Book/DVD Seminar Quantity Discounts: 2-3 (20%), 4-5 (30%), 6-9 (40%), 10+ (50%)	$399.95	
	0-9742877-0-9	Turning Struggles into Successes – Book Quantity Discounts: 1-24 (10%), 25-49 (20%), 50-74 (30%), 75+ (40%)	$29.95	
			Subtotal	
			Sales Tax (OK residents, 7.917%)	
			Total (U.S. Funds Only)	

Note: Individual copies of the book are available only with the purchase of an audio or DVD additional seminar. Additional sets of CD seminar are also available with the purchase of the audio/DVD seminar. Call for additional information.

Name _____
Address _____
City _____
State _____ Zip _____
Phone _____
E-mail _____

☐ Check or Money Order   ☐ Visa
☐ Purchase Order Attached   ☐ Mastercard

Credit Card No. _____
Expires _____
Signature _____

SATISFACTION GUARANTEED
If you are not completely satisfied with your purchase, just return the product in saleable condition within 30 days for a full refund of the purchase price.

Note: This refund offer is only valid if sealed CD/DVD envelopes have not been opened!

Order Today!

Reading Connections
PO Box 52426
Tulsa, OK 74152-0426
(918) 744-8698 Telephone
(918) 744-1052 Fax
mhoward@drmaryhoward.com